Beware!

It is unlike most any other kind of humor, for it spares no feeling or allegiance in its penetrating and cutting design. The Sick Joke is the most outrageous, insensitive, offensive and revolting brand of humor ever devised by man.

The Sick Joke

However, many people are perfect enough, or tough enough, or have a weird enough sense of humor to appreciate this kind of joke. To all others who may be too sensitive, too uncertain of their humor threshold, or just too squeamish, we caution you. . . .

This Book May Be Dangerous To Your Health!

Books by Larry Wilde

MORE The Official Democrat/Republican Joke Book
MORE The Official Smart Kids/Dumb Parents Joke Book
The Official Book of Sick Jokes
MORE The Official Jewish/Irish Joke Book
The LAST Official Italian Joke Book
The Official Cat Lovers/Dog Lovers Joke Book
The Official Dirty Joke Book
The LAST Official Polish Joke Book
The Official Golfers Joke Book
The Official Smart Kids/ Dumb Parents Joke Book
The Official Religious/NOT SO Religious Joke Book
The Official Democrat/Republican Joke Book
MORE The Official Polish/Italian Joke Book
The Official Black Folks/White Folks Joke Book
The Official Virgins/Sex Maniacs Joke Book
The Official Jewish/Irish Joke Book
The Official Polish/Italian Joke Book
The Official Bedroom/Bathroom Joke Book

also

The Complete Book of Ethnic Humor (Corwin)
How The Great Comedy Writers Create Laughter
  (Nelson-Hall)
The Great Comedians (Citadel Press)

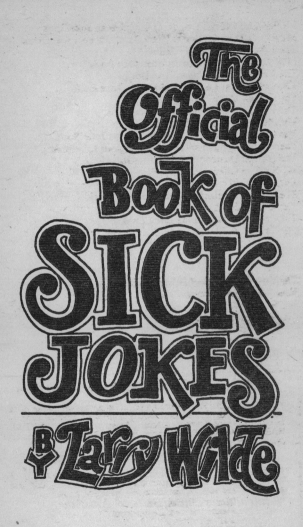

The Official Book of SICK JOKES

BY Larry Wilde

PINNACLE BOOKS   NEW YORK

For My Friend,
Andrew Ettinger,
A loving man with
A *beautiful* soul,
A *healthy* mind,
and a *sick* sense of
humor.

THE OFFICIAL BOOK OF SICK JOKES

An original Pinnacle Books edition, published for
the first time anywhere.

First printing, July 1979
Second printing, July 1979
Third printing, October 1979
Fourth printing, August 1980
Fifth printing, August 1980
Sixth printing, December 1980
Seventh printing, September 1981

ISBN: 0-523-41420-X

Printed in the United States of America

PINNACLE BOOKS, INC.
1430 Broadway
New York, New York 10018

Contents

About the Author

Larry Wilde is America's most popular joke-smith. With sales of over 4,000,000 books, his "Official" joke books have become the largest-selling humor series in the history of publishing.

Mr. Wilde's expertise in the comedic field includes a serious side. He has authored two comprehensive studies: *The Great Comedians* and *How the Great Comedy Writers Create Laughter*.

Gag lovers will also applaud the first unrestricted collection of jokes about minorities in Larry's *The Complete Book of Ethnic Humor*.

Comedian Larry Wilde has performed in the nation's finest hotels and supper clubs. He has appeared on TV with Messrs. Carson, Douglas, and Griffin, as well as on *The Comedy Shop*, a syndicated TV show featuring the country's best comics. Television audiences have also seen him as an actor on "Mary Tyler Moore," "Rhoda," "Sanford and Son," and other sitcoms and TV commercials.

Mr. Wilde is married to Maryruth Poulos, a former Wyoming beauty queen. The couple reside in Los Angeles where Larry continues to write, perform, act and lecture on the subject of comedy (while Mrs. Wilde is at work cooking, testing and assembling an unusual storehouse of recipes for her *Ethnic Homestyle Cookbook*).

INTRODUCTION

Sick Jokes shock. Many of them are so bizarre that the listener or reader actually winces before he laughs uproariously. Sick Jokes are outrageous, insensitive, and offensive but they are also very human, for life itself can be outrageous, insensitive and offensive.

Sick Jokes became a fad in the Sixties. Lenny Bruce was described as "walking softly and carrying a big sick." Mort Sahl, Tom Lehrer, Shelley Berman, Dick Gregory, Bob Newhart, et al., were accused of using gags that smacked of morbidity and downright bad taste. But Sick Jokes were around long before America's funnymen tapped the source and helped make them the nation's craze.

At various times, Sick Jokes have been referred to as Cruel Jokes, Bloody Marys,

Meanie Jokes, Depression Jokes, Hate Jokes, Sadist Jokes, Ivy League Jokes, Gruesomes, Grimsels and the Comedy of Horror.

No matter what name they go by, most Sick Jokes have in common the ridiculing of affliction. There is a callous disregard for sentiment, or tenderness or any respect for religious institutions or revered persons.

The jokes poke fun at mutilation, deformity and any physical handicap. The cripple thus takes his place beside the "moron" and the "loony" as another controversial subject for tickling the funny bone.

In *The Origins of Wit and Humor*, author Albert Rapp traces this special kind of laughter back to the caveman:

> ... *if he saw another caveman was battered, bruised, deformed or crippled in any notable way, for some inexplicable reason the former lifted his throat to the heavens and laughed.*

Burlesquing this kind of human tragedy is certainly not new. A search of literature reveals that both Cicero and Francis Bacon gave deformity a high place on their lists of causes for laughter. The princes of the Renaissance collected midgets, hunchbacks, monsters and Blackamoors for their merriment.

In the early days of English law, criminals were flogged right in the courtroom to the delight of the judge and his officers.

We have become too civilized for that kind of cruelty but children still jeer and laugh at people with a limp or stammer, at foreigners with funny pronunciation, at people oddly dressed—at any form of appearance or behavior which deviates from the norm.

Albert Rapp reports the following summary of what children laughed at after a survey:

It would be hard to find any disaster so great that it has not been a source of genuine mirth . . . severe accidents involving the greatest pain and danger to life and limb, and even death itself, may provide unquenchable laughter . . .

And what about adults?

Man seems to have moved forward in every aspect of life except in his emotions. Heart bypasses, transistors, hydrogen bombs, and astronauts on the moon, are all technological advances that testify to mankind's progress. But go to a sporting event and listen to the crowds scream for blood:

At a baseball game: "Kill the umpire!"

Basketball: "Wipe the floor with him!"

Hockey: "Cram it down his throat!"

Football: (High School Cheer)
Rip, rip, ree!
Hit him in the knee.
Rip, rip, rass
Hit him in the other knee.

In the last few years movie and TV shows depicting murder, rape, bludgeonings, violence of every sort have gained high ratings. Human beings, it seems, never tire of witnessing the maiming and killing of their fellow man.

Unquestionably, Sick Jokes are repulsive and revolting. And yet they are a part of our culture. Between these covers you will find the best and worst of the existing sick humor.

Some years ago, the brilliant satirist, Dorothy Parker, penned the following grisly lines:

4

Razors pain you;
Rivers are damp;
Acids stain you;
And drugs cause cramp.
Guns aren't lawful;
Nooses give;
Gas smells awful;
You might as well live.

Miss Parker could have added "and laugh." For, in truth, what else is there to do? Besides, it's more fun than crying. So turn the page and start laughing!

LARRY WILDE
Los Angeles, 1979

MOPPET MONKEYSHINES

"Your grandma still sliding down banisters?"

"We wound barbed wire around them."

"That stop her?"

"Nope, but it sure slows her down."

* * *

"These are Grandma's ashes."

"Oh, did the poor old lady pass away?"

"No, just too damn lazy to get an ash tray."

"Grandma, want to lose ten pounds of ugly fat?"

"Yes, dear."

"Cut off your head."

* * *

"Mommy, give us the matches?"

"Why?"

"We've got to build a fire under Danny. He swallowed the corn before we could pop it."

* * *

"Daddy, get the marshmallows quick. The baby just fell in the fire."

* * *

Did you hear about the nine-year-old boy who killed his mother and father and then pleaded with the judge for clemency because he was an orphan?

"So where is your sister?"
"Out in the barn hanging herself."
"Then go cut her down."
"Not until she is done."

*   *   *

"Can we play baseball with Harlan, Mrs. West?"
"I'm surprised at you. You know Harlan has no arms or legs."
"Yeah, but we're going to use him for 3rd base."

*   *   *

"Can Butch come out and play?"
"No, his tongue is tied."
"Well, can we come in and watch him stutter?"

*   *   *

"Fellas, can I play ping-pong?"
"You know your hooks won't hold the paddles."

"Now show Daddy exactly where you found that head."

*   *   *

"Mom, I tied Justin to a railroad track."
"Well, untie him."
"No, I like to see people with their head and body separated."

*   *   *

"You knew very well the train would run over little Homer when you put him on the tracks."
"I gave him a timetable, didn't I?"

*   *   *

Little Donald seemed to be enjoying himself thoroughly at the zoo with his father. Suddenly, as they were watching the lions, the boy looked terrified. "What's the matter?" asked his father.

"I was just wondering, Daddy. In case a lion breaks loose and eats you, what number bus do I take home?"

Little Jeffrey was sad when he found his pet turtle lying on its back on the bank of the pond. "Never mind," said his father, "we'll have a fine funeral for him. I'll make a little coffin for him and Mother will wrap him in silk. We'll buy a white picket fence to put around his grave. After we bury him we'll go down to Haägen-Dazs and I'll buy you a big ice cream cone."

Suddenly, the turtle turned over and headed for the water. "Jeff, look!" shouted his father, "Your turtle isn't dead after all!"

"Daddy, let's kill it!"

"Let's kill it!"

11

Mathews took his small son, Steven, to the art museum. When they approached a painting of the early Christian martyrs being eaten by lions, the father tried to steer the boy away. Then Mathews decided that the child would have to learn about these things sooner or later, and, taking Steven over to the picture, he began to explain, "It's only a picture. There's nothing to be afraid of. It's only a picture."

"Oh, Daddy, look!" cried the little boy.

"Now, don't be scared. It's only a picture," said Mathews.

"Ooh, look," said Steven.

"I told you, there's nothing to be frightened of."

"Look at that lion over there, Daddy," moaned the youngster.

"Well, what about him?"

"Oh, that poor lion isn't getting any."

* * *

"Mama, Mama," called Alvin, as he ran into the kitchen. "Can my friends and I borrow your curling irons? We want to play Spanish Inquisition with little Eloise!"

"Mommy, come here quickly!"

"What's the matter, dear?"

"Billy just ate the raisins off the sticky brown paper!"

* * *

"Mommy, Mommy, Daddy is throwing up all over the bathroom."

"Why are you crying, son?"

"Because Sister is getting all the big pieces."

* * *

"Come now, Arnold, and kiss your aunt."

"Why, Ma? I didn't do anything."

* * *

"Can the twins come out and play?"

"No. You know they're both in wheelchairs since the auto accident."

"Sure we do. We just wanted to roll them down hill and make book."

"Can Susan come out and play?"

"No, she is paralyzed."

"Can we come in and watch her grow stiff?"

*   *   *

"Mrs. Spencer, can Jamie come out and play?"

"Now you children know he has leprosy."

"Then can we come in and watch him rot?"

*   *   *

"Jayson, stop twisting your sister's head.

"Jayson, stop twisting your sister's head.

"For the last time, stop twisting your sister's head.

"All right, Jayson, give it back to her."

*   *   *

Little Nancy wanted to serve the tea when her mother was entertaining the Ladies Club. Her mother consented. However, she became annoyed by the long delay and asked, "Why were you so long, dear?"

"I couldn't find the tea strainer" said Nancy.

"Then how did you strain it so well?"

"I used the fly swatter."

Then there was the sadistic little girl who locked the bathroom door the night her father had his buddies over for a beer party.

*   *   *

What's red and white and comes in a test tube?
Bozo, the clone.

*   *   *

Mother: If you don't stop playing that saxophone, I'll go crazy!
Son: Too late. I stopped an hour ago.

*   *   *

"Mrs. Redman, can Christopher come to our party?"
"Of course not. You know he had an accident and broke both his legs."
"Yeah, we know. But we wanna crack our walnuts between his casts."

*   *   *

As Fritz pushed their mother over a cliff, he said, "Look Hans. No Ma."

15

"Mommy, Mommy! Daddy just poisoned my kitty."

"Don't cry dear. Maybe he had to do it."

"No, he didn't. He promised me *I* could."

*   *   *

McLeod decided it was time to lecture his young son, who was something of a screwball.

"Jimmy," he said, "you're getting to be a young man now and I think you ought to take life more seriously. Just think if I died suddenly, where would you be?"

"I'd be here," replied the kid. "The question is, where would *you* be?"

*   *   *

Adam Perlmutter, the handsome Hancock Park comic, breaks up pals with this pleaser:

The judge arraigned the little boy in court.

"You mean to tell me, young man," the judge said in disbelief, "that you shot your grandmother for 25 cents?"

"You know how it is, Judge," replied the boy. "A quarter here, a quarter there ... it adds up."

"Mom, I just knocked over the ladder in the garden."

"You'd better tell your dad."

"He knows. He was on the ladder."

* * *

"Mommy, I just put a stick of dynamite under Teacher's chair."

"That's terrible. You go right back to school and apologize."

"What school?"

* * *

A teacher was warning her pupils against catching cold. "I once had a little brother seven years old. One day he took his new sled out into the snow. He caught pneumonia and three days later he died."

A long silence and then a voice from the rear: "Where's his sled?"

* * *

"Son, will you quit kicking your sister."

"It's all right. She's already dead."

Little Marvin refused to eat. In desperation, his mother took him to a psychiatrist who tried to tempt the lad with all manner of goodies. Nothing worked. Finally, the doctor said, "All right, what would *you* like to eat?"

"Worms," replied the boy.

Not to be outsmarted, the doctor sent his nurse out for a plate of them. "Here," he said to the boy.

"I want them fried," the youngster wailed.

Again the nurse was sent out and returned with a heaping plate of fried worms.

"I only want one," yelled Marvin.

The doctor got rid of all but one. "Now," he bellowed, "eat!"

"You eat half," insisted the boy.

The doctor gagged the fried worm down, then dangled the remaining portion in Marvin's face. The boy shook with tears.

"Now what's the matter?" growled the doctor.

"You ate my half!"

"You ate my half!"

An angry mother took her nine-year-old son to the doctor's office and asked, "Is a boy of nine able to perform an appendix operation?"

"Of course not," the doctor said impatiently.

The mother turned to the boy and screamed, "So who was right? Put it back!"

* * *

Stop playing with your brother, dear.
It seems I've told you often
If you don't stop it right away
I'm gonna shut the coffin!

* * *

"Mommy, why can't I kiss Grandma?"
"Shut up, and close the casket."

* * *

"Can Rickey come out and play?"
"You know Rickey doesn't have any arms or legs."

"That's all right. We just want to put him out on the sidewalk and watch him squirm."

"Mommy, can we play with Grandpa?"
"No, you've dug him up enough already."

*   *   *

"Mommy, can I play baseball?"
"Get back in bed. You know you can't run without legs."

*   *   *

"Mommy, I want milk."
"Shut up and drink your beer."

*   *   *

"Mommy, why can't we get a garbage disposal?"
"Shut up, and start chewing."

*   *   *

"But Mother, I don't want to go to Europe."
"Shut up and get into the Care package."

*   *   *

"Daddy, can't we have a dog?"
"Shut up and keep barking."

"But Mother, I don't want to go to China."

"Shut up and keep digging."

*　　*　　*

"Daddy, why is it wrong to gamble?"

"Shut up and deal the cards."

*　　*　　*

"Mama, what is a werewolf?"

"Shut up and comb your face."

*　　*　　*

"Mother, this doesn't taste like tomato juice."

"Shut up and drink it before it clots."

*　　*　　*

"Mother, why do I have warts on me?"

"Because you are a toad, honey."

*　　*　　*

"Dad, it's dark down here."

"Shut up, or I'll flush it again."

"Mom, what are we having for supper?"

"Shut up and get back into the stove."

* * *

"Mommy, what is a cannibal?"

"Shut up and eat your brother."

* * *

"But Mother, I don't want hamburger for supper."

"Shut up and stick your arm back in the meat grinder."

* * *

"Can I go for a ride in the car?"

"No. You know your iron lung won't fit in the Volkswagen."

* * *

"Where's Mama, Daddy?"

"Drink your tomato juice."

"But where's Mama?"

"Drink your tomato juice before it coagulates."

"Mommy, can I have a new dress?"
"Of course not. You know it won't fit over your iron lung."

*　　*　　*

What's black and yellow and full of little Crispy Critters?
A burnt school bus.

*　　*　　*

"Mother, can I play the piano?"
"Of course not. You know very well your hooks will scratch the keys."

*　　*　　*

"Mrs. Hofstetter, can Craig go swimming?"
"No. You know he's got polio."
"That's all right. We want to float on his iron lung."

*　　*　　*

"Mother, can I play in the snow?
"You know your braces will rust."

"Mommy, I hate my sister's guts."

"Shut up and eat what's put in front of you."

* * *

"Mommy, can we have Grandma for dinner?"

"Shut up. We still have half of Aunt Helen in the ice box."

* * *

"Mommy, I want a new dog."

"Shut up, we haven't finished eating this one yet."

* * *

"Mommy, why are we out in our boat at night?"

"Shut up, and tie that cement block around your leg."

"But Mommy, I don't want to go swimming."

"Shut up, brat, and get back in the bag."

* * *

"Ma, I want out of the closet."

"Shut up, we don't want the fire to spread to the rest of the house."

* * *

Parker was on his way home when he passed a house and saw through the window a woman hitting a small boy over the head with a loaf of bread.

Next day he passed, and the next, and the next, and each time he saw the woman hit the boy on the head with a loaf of bread.

Finally, one Friday Parker saw her hitting the boy on the head with a cake.

"Say," he shouted through the open window, "run out of bread today?"

"Of course not," replied the woman. "It's his birthday."

"Mommy, Grandma is starting to breathe again."

"Shut up, and get that pillow back in place."

* * *

"Mommy, I fell into the well and almost drowned."

"So wipe your feet before you come in the house."

* * *

"Mommy, the power mower just cut off my foot!"

"Stay outside 'till it stops bleeding, dear. I just mopped."

* * *

"Mummy, Mummy, why can't we give Aunt Barbara's baby a proper funeral?"

"Shut up, child, and keep pulling the chain."

* * *

"Mommy, I can't move my foot."

"Shut up, or I'll cut your legs off too."

"Mommy, why do I keep walking in circles?"

"Shut up, or I'll nail your other foot to the floor."

*   *   *

"Daddy, what is a vampire?"

"Shut up and drink your blood."

"But Daddy, I don't like blood. Daddy, have a heart."

"Hmm. Think I will."

*   *   *

"Daddy, why is Mother running across the field?"

"Shut up and reload the shotgun."

*   *   *

"Uncle Spencer, Alice ate a poison mushroom!"

"I'm busy, Tommy."

"Uncle Spencer! Now Alice's fallen into the river. She's drowning!"

"The mushroom would have gotten her anyway."

"Daddy, why is Mother lying so still?"
"Shut up, and keep digging."

* * *

"I can't play archery any more."
"Lose your arrows?"
"Nope. All stuck in Mommy."

* * *

"How'd you get along with Dad while I was away?"

"Just fine. Every morning he took me down to the lake in a rowboat, and let me swim back."

"Isn't that a long distance for you to swim?"

"Oh, I always made it all right. Only trouble I had was getting out of the bag."

* * *

"Broke my kid biting his nails."
"Really? How?"
"Knocked his teeth out."

Phelps put his small son on the mantel-piece and told him to jump into his arms. When the boy jumped, his father stepped aside and the boy fell on his head.

"That'll teach you a lesson," said Phelps. "Don't trust anybody, not even your father!"

"Don't trust anybody!"

"Mommy, why are you pointing that gun at me?"
"Junior, hold still."

* * *

ASPIRIN COMMERCIAL
"Mommy, Mommy, I can't breathe!"
"Good, it's working."

* * *

"Mummy, Mummy, may I lick the bowl out?"
"No pull the chain like everyone else."

* * *

Two kids have just pushed their mother off the cliff.
1st: Let's go down and look at her mangled body.
2nd: Don't make me laugh. I've got chapped lips.

* * *

What's red and sits in the corner?
A baby chewing on razor blades.

What's blue and sits in the corner?
A baby in a Baggie.

*   *   *

What's green and sits in the corner?
The same baby a week later.

*   *   *

What's red and goes 'round and 'round?
A baby in a garbage disposal.

*   *   *

What's red and swings back and forth?
A baby on a meat hook.

*   *   *

How do you make a baby float?
A tall glass of root beer and two scoops
of baby.

What's easier to unload, a truckload of bricks or a truckload of babies?

A truckload of babies. It's tough to unload bricks with a pitchfork.

*   *   *

"How do you know your father's dead?"
"He doesn't move when I kick him."

*   *   *

"Mommy, why can't I go swimming?"
"The water's too deep."
"But Daddy's swimming!"
"He's insured."

*   *   *

"Can I play in the sandbox yet, Mommy?"
"Not until we find a better place to bury Daddy."

*   *   *

"Mama, why are we pushing the car off the cliff?"
"Shut up, or you'll wake your father."

"Hey, Ma, Alan's on fire!"

"Well, shut off the furnace. There's no use wasting coal."

* * *

"Mrs. Karas, your little boy is spoiled."

"How dare you. He is not. How dare you!"

"You should see what the steam roller just did to him."

* * *

Distressed Young Mother (on a bus with crying infant): Dear me, I just don't know what to do with this child.

Bachelor in Next Seat: Shall I open the window for you?

* * *

"Mom, Daddy just fell off the roof."

"I know, dear. I saw him pass the window."

"Mom, when will we get a garbage can?"

"Shut up and keep eating."

* * *

"Mom, Daddy is being chased by a bull."

"What can I do about it?"

"Put some film into the camera, fast!"

* * *

"My mother went down to buy a revolver."

"Did your father tell her what to get?"

"No, he doesn't even know she's going to shoot him."

* * *

"Doctor, I just swallowed my harmonica."

"Calm down and be glad you didn't play the piano."

* * *

"I want some rat poison."

"Should I wrap it up or do you want to eat it here?"

"Eustace!" called Mama, "are you spitting into that fish bowl?"

"No, Ma, but I'm coming closer with every try."

* * *

Mother: Well, children, what have you been doing while I've been out shopping?

Children: Oh, Mommy, we've been having so much fun! We've got Granny's hearing aid up to 50,000 watts—and you should see her nose glow!

* * *

"Mommy, are you sure this is the way to make pizza?"

"Shut up and get back in the oven."

* * *

"Why are my teeth so long, Daddy?"

"Shut up and drink your blood!"

* * *

Horace was a noisy child,
He nearly drove his parents wild,
Until his father, Dr. Fords,
Dissected out his vocal cords.

37

"Mother, can I go ice skating?"

"No, dear, skates won't fit your crutches."

* * *

Little Cindy: Grandma, can you eat nuts?
Grandma: No, my dear, I have no teeth!
Little Cindy: Good. Then you can mind the pecans till I get back.

* * *

Little Raymond had been blind since birth. One day, at bedtime, his mother told him she had a wonderful surprise for him tomorrow. If he followed her suggestions he would be able to see for the first time in his life. She told him to pray very hard for sight.

The next morning she asked him if he prayed and he said he did. She said, "Raymond, when you open your eyes you'll be able to see because your prayers have been answered."

Raymond opened his eyes but he was still blind. He cried: "Mother, Mother, I can't see, I can't see."

She said, "I know, dear. April Fool."

GROWN-UP GROANERS

"You drove one of your passengers to a secluded spot, strangled him, and dismembered his body. What have you got to say for yourself?"

"Who's going to pay the cab fare?"

* * *

Pete: Whisper those three little words that will make me walk on air.

Jane: Go hang yourself.

* * *

"But Warden, I like Joe."

"Shut up and pull the switch."

Did you hear about the man with two wooden legs whose house caught on fire?

He was burned to the ground.

* * *

Paxton was explaining that he had found a sure-fire method for putting the baby to sleep.

"I toss it up in the air again and again."

"How does that put it to sleep?" asked his neighbor.

"We have very low ceilings."

* * *

The tailor called Toulouse-Lautrec and left a message with his valet: "Tell Mr. Lautrec his tailor called—his Bermuda shorts are ready."

40

"What do you mean your wooden legs hurt you? You can't feel pain in a wooden leg."

"You don't understand. During the fight with this man—he hit me over the head with it."

* * *

The Gladwells had a baby born without ears. They brought it home and their neighbors, the Petersons, were preparing to visit it. "Now, please be careful," said Mrs. Peterson to her husband, "don't say anything about the baby not having any ears."

"Don't worry," said Peterson. "I won't do anything to hurt their feelings."

So they went next door, up into the nursery and stood over the new baby's crib with the Gladwells. "He's so cute," said Mrs. Peterson to the baby's mother.

"Yeah," agreed Mr. Peterson. "What strong arms and legs the kid has—he's gonna grow up to be a bruiser."

"Thanks," said the baby's father.

"How's the kid's eyes?"

"They're perfect!" said Gladwell.

"They'd better be! He won't ever be able to wear any glasses!"

"How'd you blow that tire?"

"Ran over a milk bottle."

"Didn't you see it?"

"Damn kid had it under his coat."

*   *   *

Unfortunately, Willard's head was about twice the size it should be. His little classmates invented offensive nicknames for him, and finally he refused to go to school at all. His mother tried to reassure him: "Your head's no bigger than any of the other kids, and, in fact, you're the handsomest boy in the school. Now you just cheer up and go down to the grocery store and bring home five dozen bottles of ginger ale."

"I've got nothing to carry them in," said Willard.

"Don't be silly," said the mother. "Use your hat!"

*   *   *

RECRUITING POSTER
Today's Army Won't Cost You An Arm and a Leg

"I finally stopped my roommate from biting his nails."

"How?"

"I made him wear shoes."

*   *   *

The German family was out having a picnic. Mama Hilda was spreading out the food when suddenly a huge rock came tumbling down the hill and landed right on Papa Ludvig, killing him instantly.

Turning to the children, Hilda said happily, "Well, that's all the more for us then!"

*   *   *

For the fourteenth time, Mrs. Jenkins led her small son to the ticket window of the railroad station and asked, "Will you please tell me what time the next train goes to Springdale."

The hair-lipped ticket agent replied, "Madam, I told you fourteen times it goes at five o'clock. Will you stop annoying me!"

"Well, mister, I wouldn't bother you so much, but it makes my little boy laugh to hear you talk."

A murder victim was lying on the street in a pool of blood when two artists came along.

"What should we do?" asked one.

"Fingerpaint, man, fingerpaint," said the other.

* * *

"Excuse me, Mrs. Yates, my daughter has lost her arrow."

"Where is it?"

"I think it's stuck in your son."

* * *

Greenberg and Murphy were fishing in separate boats some distance apart. The Irishman got a bite and was so nervous that he fell out of the boat.

He sank twice, and as he came up the second time, Greenberg rowed over and called out, "Mister, can I have your boat if you don't come up again?"

Schneider's wife gave birth to a baby, so he went to the hospital to see it. He followed Miss Norton into a room and spotted a beautiful healthy baby. "Oh, how beautiful," he exclaimed.

"That's not your baby," said Miss Norton.

She took him into another room and in a crib lay a tiny, deformed infant. Schneider stared at it and said, "That's okay, I'll still love it."

"No, no," cried the nurse, "that's not yours."

They went into an adjacent room where there was just a head resting on a pillow. "Oh, well," resigned Schneider, "it's still my baby and I'll love it."

"Sorry," said Miss Norton, "that's not yours either."

They stepped into a nearby room and there lying in the center of a table was just an eye. "All right," sobbed Schneider, "it's just an eye but I'll still love it with all my heart."

"Okay, Mr. Schneider, but I thought you'd just like to know that it's blind."

Judy Cassayre, the remarkable Rams Head Realty exec at Sea Ranch, California, relates this rib-buster:

The governor of a Midwestern state was in San Francisco to give a political speech. Up in his room, the politician, as always, was having great difficulty tying his tuxedo tie. So he looked out into the hotel hallway and saw a stranger passing by. "Would you mind helping me with this tie? It always gives me trouble."

"Not at all," said the man, "but I'm afraid you'll have to lie down on the bed."

The governor thought this was a peculiar way of tying a bow tie but he complied. When the tie was properly adjusted, the governor said, "How come you can't tie this unless I lie down?"

"I'm an undertaker," said the man.

"*I'm an undertaker!*"

47

Monte Mellman, discount appliance mogul, manufactured this mouthful:

Elsdon walked into a bar, ordered a drink and noticed a man lying on the floor. He picked him up and propped him on a stool. A minute later the man was on the floor again. Elsdon repeated his kindness but the man again fell off the stool.

"Hey," said Elsdon to the bartender, "this guy is so out of it I better take him home."

Elsdon looked through his pockets for identification and discovered the guy lived all the way over on the other side of town. But being the good Samaritan he was, Elsdon loaded the guy in his car and drove him home.

They arrived at the man's building. Elsdon leaned the fella up against the wall while he rang the bell. But the guy fell down again. Once more, Elsdon picked him up. Just then the door opened and a woman said, "Oh, that's my husband."

"I'm glad to hear that, lady," said Elsdon.

"Thank you for bringing him home. But where's his wheel chair?"

"I made a killing in the market today."

"Really?"

"Yeah, I shot the manager of the A & P."

* * *

NEWSPAPER AD
Man to work as garbage collector
$200 a week and all you can eat

* * *

"My husband is an angel."

"You mean he finally reformed?"

"No, he went looking for a gas leak with a match."

* * *

"Hey!" cried Satan to the arrival. "You act as if you own the place."

"I do," came the reply. "My wife gave it to me before I died."

ROMAN POLANSKI'S LATEST FILM
Close Encounters with the Third Grade

* * *

A woman driver ran over a cripple crossing the street. Horrified, she stopped and called:

"Oh, dear. What can I do to help?"

"Just don't back up."

* * *

"Ma'am, your husband has just been run over by a steamroller!"

"I'm in the tub. Slip him under the door."

* * *

"Now, sir. You've applied for a job as a railroad switchman. What would you do if you saw two trains approaching each other on the same track?"

"I'd throw the lever and switch onto another track."

"And if the lever was jammed?"

"I'd turn the signals to red by hand."

"And if the signals were jammed?"

"I'd grab a red flag and run out on the track."

"And if the engineers didn't see you?"

"I'd send for my sister."

"Your sister? What could she do?"

"Nothing. She just loves to watch train wrecks."

*　　*　　*

Lawyers have a particular way of expressing themselves. They'll never come right out and say, "My client is guilty. He told me so." Here's a typical lawyer's plea to a jury:

"My client is alleged to have killed his wife. He is supposed to have chopped up her body into little pieces, and stuffed them into a suitcase. He was apprehended trying to cross the border into Mexico when someone noticed that a piece of her thumb was sticking out of the suitcase.

"Now ladies and gentlemen of the jury, I know what you're thinking. You're thinking my client is a beast, he's a killer, he's a maniac. Well, I don't see him that way. A sloppy packer, maybe. . . ."

Paul and his wife were seated at the dinner table when the doorbell rang. Paul went to the door. The visitor said, "I'm the Boston Strangler."

Paul yelled back to his wife, "It's for you, dear."

* * *

"My whole family was sort of strange, Doc," admitted the patient.

"What do you mean?" asked the psychiatrist.

"Well, take my brother. Once when we were kids, we were playing outside. It was his birthday. He tripped and fell down a dry well."

"That certainly is sad," admitted the doctor, "but why do you think it's strange?"

"When we lowered his birthday cake down to him, he didn't even tug on the rope to say thanks."

* * *

The bandage-covered patient who lay in the hospital bed spoke dazedly to his visiting pal.

"Wh-wh-what happened?"

"You had one too many last night and then bet that you could jump out the window and fly around the block."

"Why didn't you stop me?" he screamed.

"Stop you, hell. I had $25 on you."

* * *

Dawson was told by his doctor that he had to stop drinking. To overcome the craving, the M.D. suggested he eat something every time he felt like taking a drink. Dawson tried it. Each time he felt the need of some he ate some food instead. And it worked.

One night, while at a hotel, Dawson heard a strange sound in the next room and climbed on a chair to look through the transom. He was shocked to see a man hanging himself.

Dawson rushed down the stairs, and grabbed the hotel clerk. "S-s-say," he stammered, "there's a fella in the room next to mine. He's hanging himself. I saw him. For God's sake, give me a plate of ham and eggs!"

"You get the number of the woman who ran you over?"

"No, but I'd recognize that laugh anywhere."

* * *

"How come your father's so mad about us using his car last night?"

"That was him we ran down."

* * *

Grant came home and said to his wife, "Honey, I've got good news and bad news."

"What's the good news?" asked Mrs. Grant.

"I'm getting $50,000 severance pay?"

"And the bad news?"

"Wait'll you hear what they severed!"

* * *

"I just made out my will at the lawyer's."

"Why do you look so happy?"

"I believe in giving even after death. I donated my eyes to the blind, my ears to the deaf, and my ass to the Gay Liberation Movement."

* * *

Hoffman got into a bad auto accident and his face was so badly damaged he had to have skin grafts.

"Where did the skin come from?" asked a friend.

"I don't know," he replied, "but it's funny—every time I get tired, my face wants to sit down."

* * *

Mark had only one eye. He married Stella and on their wedding night discovered she was not a virgin. "You have not come to me complete!" he screamed angrily.

"Neither have you," she replied, referring to his missing eye.

"My enemies did that to me!" said Mark.

"And my friends did this to me!" said Stella.

FROM A SUNDAY SCHOOL
SCHOLAR

The Romans gave up their big holidays because of the terrific overhead. The lions ate up all their prophets.

*　　*　　*

Old farmer Hunsley and his wife were listening to the faith healer on the radio: "All you people in Radioland, with God's help I want to heal you—put one hand on the radio and one hand on the part that needs healing, and get ready."

The old lady put one hand on the radio and the other on her heart. Hunsley put one hand on the radio and the other on his tired old tool.

When Mrs. Hunsley saw this she said, "No, Elmer—he said heal the sick, not raise the dead!"

*　　*　　*

I got a dog, his name is Rover.
He's fluffy and soft and brown all over.
He's as cute and cuddly as sugar babies.
It's sure too bad that he's got rabies.

"There's one thing I haven't lost!"

A farmer, who was a witness in a railroad case in Vermont, was asked to tell in his own way how the accident happened.

"Well, Zeke and me was walkin' down the track and I heered a whistle and I got off the track; and the train went by, and I got back on the track and I didn't see Zeke; but I walked along, and pretty soon I seen Zeke's hat, and I walked on and seen one of Zeke's legs, and then I seen one of Zeke's arms, and then another leg, and then over on one side was Zeke's head, and I says, 'By cracky, something musta happened to Zeke.' "

* * *

Facing each other in court were McAlister, the tenant, and Mrs. Hanrahan, the landlady who was demanding his eviction.

"This is an open and shut case, Judge," said McAlister. "She just doesn't agree with my religious beliefs."

"My good lady," said the judge, "you can't evict a man just because you are of different faiths. We are living in a democracy, and the cornerstone of democracy is tolerance."

"It wasn't so much that I objected to his beliefs, Your Honor," explained the landlady. "When I got mad was when he wanted to sacrifice a black bull to Jupiter—right on my new rug!"

* * *

Dobbins lost his eye in an accident and couldn't afford the price of a glass eye. So he carved one out of wood. But he was so self-conscious that he never left the house.

Finally, his friend Eddy came over and forced him to go out. "There's a dance over at the club," he said. "So one of your eyes is made out of wood, so what?"

"All right," said Dobbins, "but if anybody makes fun of my eye I'm leaving."

He went to the dance and stood around, trying to build up his courage. And then he saw Ellen, standing alone in the corner. Ellen was very attractive, but she had a hunchback. "She's worse off than I am," Dobbins thought. "The least I can do is ask her to dance."

He walked across the crowded dance floor and approached the girl. "Would you care to dance?" he asked.

"Would I!" she exclaimed.

"That does it!" he shouted, *"Hunchback! Hunchback!"*

District Attorney: Now tell the jury the truth. Why did you shoot your husband with a bow and arrow?

Defendant: I didn't want to wake the children.

* * *

"Pilot to tower. Out of gas three hundred miles over Atlantic. Request instructions."

"Tower to pilot. Repeat after me. Our Father, who art in heaven. . ."

* * *

A traveling salesman's car broke down. After walking for several hours, he spotted a mountaineer's shack. He knocked on the door and a bearded man with a shotgun appeared.

"My car has stalled and I was wondering if I could spend the night?" he asked, chuckling inwardly as he awaited the inevitable answer.

"Wal," drawled the mountaineer, "you could sleep with my daughter, but she's in an iron lung."

Three wise men entered the manger where the newborn baby lay. The first and second wise men presented their gifts and made compliments on how the baby looked. As the third gave his gift he tripped over a board and in pain howled, "Jesus Christ!"

Mary said, "Now that's a good name for the baby!"

*   *   *

Perce walked in to where the Last Supper was being held, sat down at the table and said to the waiter, "Give me a scotch and soda!"

"I'm sorry, sir," said the waiter, "all we're serving is wine."

"Okay. Give me a nice thick steak with a baked potato and a salad."

"Sorry, but all we're serving is bread."

"Holy mackerel! Only bread and wine! The guy who's giving this party ought to be crucified!"

The angry mob was about to stone the prostitute to death when Jesus intervened. "Let him who is without sin cast the first stone," he said. Ashamed, the crowd began to break up. Suddenly, a little old lady picked up a jagged rock and hit the prostitute right between the eyes. Jesus glared at the old woman, stalked over and said, "Sometimes, Mother, you really piss me off!"

*   *   *

"George, George, those diamonds are lovely."

"Shut up and keep running. The cops are gaining on us."

*   *   *

"Emily, I told you the plane didn't have a powder room."

"Shut up and pull the rip cord."

*   *   *

Tonto: Me no like your horse, Silver.
Lone Ranger: Keep quiet and eat.

"My grandfather believed in reincarnation."

"Is that right?"

"In fact, his will called for his unexpired magazine subscriptions to be forwarded to the cemetery."

* * *

The latest rock 'n roll record is "Stomping at the Crucifix," by Pontius Pilate and the Nasty Nail Drivers.

* * *

The Sunday gospel shouter was in great form.

"Everything God has made is perfect," he preached.

A small, gnarled hunchback rose in the rear of the auditorium and asked, "What about me?"

"Why," responded the preacher, "you're the most perfect hunchback I ever saw."

SIMTHEREENS SONATA

My bonnie looked into the gas tank,
The height of its contents to see.
She lit a small match to assist her—
Oh, bring back my bonnie to me.

* * *

An absent-minded professor was conducting a class in zoology and addressing the students. He said, "Now this morning we will take this frog apart and see what makes him croak."

He took a paper bag out of his pocket, then emptied the contents on his desk. Out rolled a ham sandwich. He scratched his head and said, "That's odd. I distinctly remember eating my lunch."

* * *

"I guess I've lost another pupil," said the professor as his glass eye rolled down the sink.

"Mother, may I have a new dress for Easter?"

"Certainly not, Richard!"

*　　*　　*

Hiram, the farm boy, was too bashful to tell Lulubelle he loved her, yet he wanted desperately to marry her. Finally, he blurted out, "Lulu, how would you like to be buried with my people?"

*　　*　　*

"The Poles have just recruited a special new elite fighting force to send to Africa."

"What's so special about them?"

"They're all epileptics."

"Isn't that kind of silly?"

"No, the enemy can't tell which ones have already been shot."

Cusick and Waznicki were strolling in the woods. Suddenly Cusick, said "Look, there's Zelda's left arm. I'm sure that's the bracelet she wore."

Plunging farther into the forest, Waznicki exclaimed, "Say, there's Zelda's right arm. I'd know that wristwatch anywhere."

Continuing their journey, they met up with Zelda's right leg, her left leg, her torso, and finally they arrived at a spot where Zelda's dismembered head looked up at them. "Hey," said Cusick, "there's Zelda now."

Waznicki picked up the head and held it at arm's length. "No," he said, "Zelda was a much taller girl!"

"*Zelda was much taller!*"

Alma and Nick had a baby. Unfortunately, it was born without arms, or legs or even a torso. There was just a head. Still, they loved it. Nursed it, cared for it, loved it for 20 years. They finally decided to go to Europe for a vacation.

At a cocktail party they met a doctor whom they described their son to. He said, "Amazing. But I have been working on a way to help your son. I can attach arms, and legs and a body to his head."

Alma and Nick flew back home, raced into their house and into the nursery. Alma looked down into the crib where the head lay and said, "Sonny, Mommy and Daddy have the most wonderful surprise for you!"

"Oh, my God!" shouted the head, "not another hat!"

* * *

Once upon a time, the king of a far-off country offered a thousand gold coins and a large parcel of land to anyone who could bring him a new and delicious fruit. From all over the world, men came bearing papayas, guavas, mangos, coconuts, and all other exotic fruits. But the king turned them all down.

Then, finally, young Amesbury made his offering. The king tasted it and shouted. "That's it! What do you call this?"

"These are raisins, my lord."

"You shall have the reward," said the king, "if you will but bring me raisins every day."

And so Amesbury brought the king raisins every day, year in and year out. Then one morning the young man did not bring raisins.

"What is this?" demanded the king.

"Peaches, my lord."

"Why have you not brought raisins?"

"Well," said Amesbury, "my rabbit died."

*   *   *

The Hubbards, a husband and wife, both 92 years old, stood before a judge, wanting a divorce.

"I don't understand," said the magistrate, "after all these years of being married why would you want to get a divorce?"

"Well, answered the old man, "we wanted to wait until the children died."

Martial law had been established in a small South American country. Everybody had to be home by 9:00. Two soldiers were standing in the city square when they spotted a drunk weaving his way up the street. One of the men took aim and shot him.

"Why did you kill that poor drunk? It's only five minutes to nine."

"I know where he lives and he'd never make it home in five minutes."

* * *

CALIFORNIA BUMPER STICKER
Support Mental Health—or I'll Kill You!

* * *

"They've got bottomless waiters now in San Francisco."

"No kidding."

"Well, actually they're amputees pushing themselves around on those little rollers."

Doctor Rogers made a clone of himself. Unfortunately, it didn't turn out too well. The clone was ugly. In fact it was obscene. The M.D. hated it so much he took it to a cliff and pushed it off.

But the police got wind of what he was going to do and actually saw him get rid of the clone. "You're under arrest," shouted the Captain.

"You can't arrest me," shouted the doctor. "I didn't kill anyone."

"That may be so," answered the police officer, "but we're arresting you for making an obscene clone fall."

* * *

"Why'd you have your mother cremated?"

"I'm gonna keep her in a big jar on the kitchen shelf. Now every morning I can have a cup of Instant Mother for breakfast."

* * *

WACKY WILLIES

Years ago, "Getting the Willies" meant having a bad case of nerves, a feeling of uneasiness. The expression evolved from a form of macabre humor known as Little Willies. These ditties first appeared in an English collection called Ruthless Rhymes for Heartless Homes, *by Harry Graham, in 1899. Graham created many of them, but with instant popular acclaim they soon proliferated into thousands. Here are some of the best:*

Little Willie found a looking glass
And scraped the mercury all off;
He swallowed the shining substance
Thinking it would cure his cough.

The next day when his mother
Told her neighbor, Mrs. Brown,
She said, "T'was a very cold day for
Willie
When the mercury went down!"

* * *

Willie, whose ideas are strange,
Put some pinwheels in the range.
When Mom lit the gas next day,
Boy! It was some grand display!!!

* * *

Willie, when the wind was strong,
Flew his kite all morning long.
"My," he cried, "just see it dance!
The tail's made out of Papa's pants."

* * *

Willie, writing on the bed,
Spilt some ink on Mother's spread.
"Ma," he said, when she came back,
"It will dye a lovely black!"

Willie playfully poisoned his Ma;
When he'd finished his work,
He remarked with a smirk,
"This will cause quite a family jar."

*　*　*

Willie split the baby's head,
To see if brains were gray or red.
Mother, troubled, said to Father,
"Children are an awful bother!"

*　*　*

Little Willie, raising hob,
Laughed at Mother's boyish-bob.
Mercy! How his trousers tingled
When he, later on, was shingled!

*　*　*

Willie caught his sister, Nan,
Being hugged by her young man.
"Gee!" said Willie, with a cackle,
"That guy don't know how to tackle."

74

Little Willie, with a rock,
Beaned the cuckoo in the clock.
Father said: "Why don't it tick?"
Willie said: "The bird is sick."

* * *

Willie scalped his baby brother,
Left him lying hairless;
"Willie," said his worried mother,
"You are getting careless."

* * *

Willie, hitting at a ball,
Lined one down the schoolhouse hall.
Through his door came Dr. Hill.
Several teeth are missing still.

* * *

Little Willie lit a rocket
Which his pa had in his pocket.
Next day he told Uncle Dan,
"Papa is a traveling man."

Little Willie, on his bike,
Through the village took a hike.
Mrs. Thompson blocked the walk;
She will live, but still can't talk.

* * *

Willie poisoned Father's tea;
Father died in agony.
Mother came, and looked quite vexed:
"Really, Will," she said, "what next?"

* * *

Little Willie on the track
Heard the engine squeal.
Now the engine's coming back;
They're scraping Willie off the wheel.

* * *

Willie's pa, I grieve to state,
Came home from the lodge quite late.
When he tottered Willie cried,
"Look at Papa! He's off-side!"

Little Willie, home from school,
Where he'd learned the Golden Rule,
Said, "If I eat up this cake
Sis won't have a stomach ache."

* * *

Willie and two other brats
Licked up all the Rough-on-Rats.
Father said, when Mother cried,
"Never mind—they'll die outside."

* * *

Willie, cunning little creature,
Blew a bean and hit his teacher.
"Most impressive was the scene,"
Willie said, "when bean met bean."

* * *

Willie, at a passing gent,
Threw a batch of fresh cement
Crying, "Wait until you dry,
Then you'll be a real hard guy."

* * *

Willie, as the fire burned low,
Gave it a terrific blow.
Grandpa's beard got in the draft;
Dear me, how the firemen laughed!

Into the cistern little Willie
Pushed his little sister Lily.
Mother couldn't find our daughter;
Now we sterilize our water.

* * *

The following are in the "Willie" tradition but are broadened to include the names of other family members:

In the deep, deep drinking well
Which the plumber built her,
Dear Aunt Eliza fell—
We must buy a filter.

* * *

Baby sat on the window seat,
Mary pushed Baby into the street.
Baby's brains splattered the "airy"
And Mother smiled, "*tch, tch,*" at Mary.

* * *

O'er the rugged mountain's brow
Clara threw the twins she nursed,
And remarked, "I wonder now
Which will reach the bottom first?"

Auntie, did you feel no pain
Falling from that apple tree?
Would you do it, please, again!
'Cos my friend here didn't see.

* * *

I had written to Aunt Maud,
Who was on a trip abroad,
When I heard she'd died of cramp—
Just too late to save the stamp.

* * *

Father, I regret to state,
Cut his daughters up for bait,
We miss them when it's time to dine.
But Father's fish taste simply fine.

* * *

Sam had spirits naught could check,
And today, at breakfast, he
Broke his baby sister's neck,
So he shant's have jam for tea!

Father heard his children scream,
So he threw them in the stream;
Saying, as he drowned the third,
"Children should be seen, *not* heard!"

*   *   *

Pity now poor Mary Ames,
Blinded by her brother James;
Hot nails in her eyes he poked—
I ne'er saw Mary more provoked.

*   *   *

Baby Bobby in the tub;
Ma forgot to place the plug;
Oh what sorrow! Oh what pain!
There goes Bobby down the drain.

*   *   *

Father nailed his darling wife
Fast against the parquet flooring.
He was loath to take her life,
But he had to stop her snoring.

My darling wife was always glum.
I drowned her in a cask of rum,
And so made sure that she would stay
In better spirits night and day.

* * *

Help! Murder! Police!
My wife fell down in grease;
I laughed so hard, I fell in the lard.
Help! Murder! Police!

* * *

When Grandmama fell off the boat
And couldn't swim, and wouldn't float,
Matilda just stood by and smiled.
I very nearly slapped the child.

* * *

MAIMED MIRTH

"Gosh, Dad, was that Reggie Jackson who just hit that home run?"

"What do you care, Sheldon? You're blind."

* * *

"Have you seen Stevie Wonder's new car?"

"No."

"Neither has he."

"I'm afraid I've got some bad news for you," the obstetrician told the new father. "Your wife has just given birth to a seven-pound, three-ounce eye."

"My God, that's terrible. That's the worst news I've ever heard."

"That's not the half of it," said the doctor, "It's blind."

*   *   *

Did you hear about the guy who gave Ray Charles a ticket to go see Marcel Marceau?

*   *   *

"Mommy, who turned out the light?"
"Shut up, you know you're blind."

*   *   *

Mangled pedestrian: What's the matter, are you blind?
Motorist: Blind? I hit ya, didn't I?

Brewster answered an ad for a bartender. "You can have the job," said the owner. "The only thing is, all my customers are deaf and dumb."

"That's okay with me," said Brewster.

"Just remember when they hold up one finger that means they want a beer. Two fingers means a shot of whiskey. And when they wave a hand around their heads it means they want to buy a round of drinks for everybody."

The boss left Brewster behind the bar. As the evening wore on the bar became packed with deaf mutes. Brewster filled their orders patiently. One finger for a beer. Two for whiskey. Hand wave around the head, he served a round for everybody.

Around 11:00 one deaf mute stood up, opened his mouth, shook his head and waved his hands. Brewster didn't understand what the man wanted. Suddenly, another mute did the same thing. Then another and another. Soon every man at the bar was waving his hands and shaking his head with his mouth opened.

Brewster phoned the boss, "What am I gonna do? I don't know what that means."

"Oh, don't worry about it," said the owner. "They're just singing!"

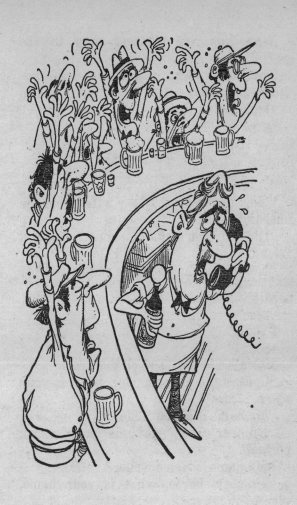

"They're singing!"

Who was the meanest man in the world?

The fellow who raped the deaf-and-dumb girl, then cut off her fingers so she couldn't yell for help.

* * *

"Now I'm taller than my wife," said the husband gleefully.

"Did you get elevator shoes?" asked a friend.

"No, she just had her legs amputated."

* * *

Helen Keller on "To Tell the Truth":

"Contestant Number One, what is your name, please?"

"My name is Helen Keller."

"Number Two, what is your name, please?"

"My name is Helen Keller."

"Number Three, what is your name, please?"

"Bluh waqf btyx krojv narf."

How did Helen Keller burn her fingers?
Trying to read a waffle iron.

*   *   *

How did Helen Keller go crazy?
Trying to read a stucco wall.

*   *   *

How did Helen Keller burn her face?
She tried to answer the iron.

*   *   *

How did Helen Keller's parents punish her?
They re-arranged the furniture.

*   *   *

What did Helen Keller's parents do when they caught her swearing?
They washed her hands with soap.

*   *   *

How did Helen Keller burn her face?
Bobbing for french fries.

What did Helen Keller do when she fell down a well?
She yelled and yelled for help 'til her hands turned blue.

*　　*　　*

Why does Helen Keller only use one hand to masturbate with?
She uses the other hand to moan with!

*　　*　　*

Did you hear about Helen Keller?
She jumped off a bridge and screamed her fingers off.

*　　*　　*

HELEN KELLER'S NEW BOOK
Around the Block in 80 Days

*　　*　　*

Why were Helen Keller's hands purple?
She heard it from the grape vine.

*　　*　　*

What is Helen Keller's favorite song?
"The Sound of Sound."

LOONEY LAFFS

Two inmates of a Michigan mental institution were chatting in the recreation room. The first looney said, "Don't talk to me, I am Napoleon!"

"What do you mean, you're Napoleon?" asked the second nut.

"I told you not to speak to me. I am Napoleon."

"How do you know you're Napoleon?"

"God told me I am Napoleon."

A little voice from the corner piped, "I did not!"

Some visitors to an insane asylum were being shown around by a guard. "You see that man over there?" said the guard. "He thinks he is the Lord."

One of the visitors approached the lunatic and asked, "Did you really make the earth in seven days?"

The nut sneered at him, "I'm not in the mood to talk shop!"

*　　*　　*

Jimmy Carter was visiting one of the largest institutions for the mentally unbalanced. He finished inspecting the main building and wanted to see the Farm Section. His chauffeur wasn't around, so the President boarded the regular bus. In a few minutes the Keeper brought on some inmates. When they were seated he began counting, "1, 2, 3, 4, 5 . . ." He got to the President and said, "Who are you?"

Mr. Carter said, "Why, I'm the President of the United States!"

The Keeper said, "6, 7, 8 . . ."

*　　*　　*

A farmer was driving by an asylum with a load of fertilizer. One of the boobies looked through the fence and yelled, "What have you got there?"

The farmer said, "Some fertilizer."

The looney said, "What are you gonna do with it?"

The farmer said, "Put it on strawberries!"

He said, "You'd better come in here, we put sugar and cream on ours!"

*　　*　　*

"Why don't you go up and turn that light on?" said Greer, a funny farm inmate.

"Can't," answered his friend, Slocum. "Don't have a ladder!"

"You don't need one," said Greer. "Just climb up the beam of my flashlight."

"Oh, no," exclaimed Slocum, "I'll get half-way up and you'll turn your flashlight off!"

*　　*　　*

One of the inmates was sitting on a chair, holding a fishing pole with a hook in a basin of water. Another inmate asked, "You catch anything?"

He said, "Are you crazy? This is just a basin of water!"

This lovely dash of whimsical lunacy was told magnificently to audiences all over America by the multi-faceted funnyman Jan Murray:

Keeler was walking out of an asylum when he noticed an inmate sitting on the lawn with a can of paint, painting the grass green.

"Hey," shouted the inmate, "don't you recognize me?"

"No," answered Keeler, watching the man painting the grass green.

"I'm your old friend Rob Morton. My family had me committed to steal my money. But I've got $50,000 hidden away in a tin box. If you get it for me I'll give you half."

"$25,000? What do I have to do?"

"Look," said the looney. "Walk up the road, turn left for three miles, you'll see an oak tree with a shovel leaning against it. Pick up the shovel, walk 40 paces to your right, 30 paces to your left and at that point dig down 20 feet. You'll find a little tin box with $50,000 in it. You keep 25, bring the rest back to me."

Keeler walked up to the road, turned left for three miles, and found the big oak tree with a shovel leaning against it. He picked up the shovel, walked 40 paces to his right, 30 paces to his left, at that point dug down 20 feet—no tin box. He dug down 40 feet, no money—three days later—no box. Keeler ran back to the asylum and found Morton sitting on the lawn painting the grass green.

"Hey, you sent me on a wild goose chase. I did everything you told me and I couldn't find the money."

"Did you turn left for three miles at the big oak tree?" asked Morton.

"Yes!"

"Did you pick up the shovel and walk 40 paces to your right?"

"Yes!"

"Thirty paces to your left, at that point dig down 20 feet?"

"Yes!"

"O.K. Grab a brush!"

* * *

A lunatic escaped from the insane asylum and went on a rampage, raping half a dozen women. The next day the newspaper headlines read:

NUT BOLTS AND SCREWS

A new inmate checked into a California asylum. He seemed quite happy. In fact, he was laughing uproariously.

"Nearest kin?" asked the examining physician.

"Twin brother," responded the fellow. "We were identical twins. Couldn't tell us apart. In school, he'd throw a spitball and the teacher would blame me. Once he was arrested for speeding and the judge fined me. I had a girl; he ran off with her."

"Then why are you laughing?"

" 'Cause I got even with him last week."

"What happened?"

"I died and they buried him."

*   *   *

Ralters came up for parole. They told him if he answered just one question sanely, he'd be released. Doctor Kole, the psychiatrist, asked him, "What would be your first action on being released from this asylum?"

Ralters said, "I'd take a sling shot and knock out all the windows in this building!"

He was sent back to his cell.

Six months later Ralters again came up

for parole and Dr. Kole asked him, "What would be the first thing you'd do upon being released from this institution?"

He said, "Well, I'd buy myself a new suit!"

"Then what would you do?"

"I'd call up a blonde I know!"

"And after that?"

"I'd take her to a motel."

"That's fine, then what?"

"I'd lock the door, sit her on the bed, run my hand up her stocking, rip off her pantyhose, make a slingshot, and knock out all the windows in this building!"

*　　*　　*

Bixby was pushing a wheelbarrow full of sand down Woodward Avenue in Detroit. He stopped every four feet and sprinkled several handfuls of sand on the pavement. "Hey, what're you doin'?" asked a policeman.

"I gotta do this," explained Bixby, "it keeps the crocodiles away."

"Wait a minute," said the cop, "there ain't any crocodiles around here."

"See," said the sand sprinkler, "this stuff really works."

Kress was standing in his cell completely nude except for a top hat on his head. The guard said to him, "How come you're not wearing any clothes?"

He said, "No one ever comes in here!"

"Well, what are you wearing a hat for?"

"Someone might!" said the looney.

*　　*　　*

Swales entered the psychiatrist's office, sat down in a chair, took a tobacco pouch from his pocket and began stuffing pipe tobacco into his left ear.

"Well, Mr. Swales," said the analyst, "you've certainly come to the right place. How can I help you?"

"Have you got a light?"

*　　*　　*

A visiting psychiatrist, wandering through the wards of a state asylum, saw a patient huddled in a corner scratching himself incessantly.

"Excuse me," said the doctor, "why do you scratch yourself like that?"

"Because," replied the man, "I'm the only one who knows where I itch."

Pennock went to his doctor complaining bitterly that he had an eggplant growing out of his right nostril.

"You must be terribly upset," said the doctor.

"You bet I am, Doc," said the patient. "I hate eggplant. I planted radishes."

* * *

"Doctor, I don't know why I'm here. My wife insisted that I talk to you because she thinks there's something wrong with me."

"What makes her think that?" inquired the psychiatrist.

"I don't know," said the patient, "except she sort of resents the way I love pancakes."

"That's ridiculous. I love pancakes too."

"No kidding, Doc? Why don't you come over to my house this evening. I have a whole basement full of them."

* * *

"Doctor, what can I do about these little green men crawling all over me?"

"Just don't brush any on me," said the shrink.

Andy Goldberg, Houston's top young athlete, breaks up buddies with this hunk of hysteria:

Summerville had been seeing a shrink three times a week for several years. As he finished his last session, Summerville pulled out a gun, pointed it at the analyst and said, "You've helped me a hell of a lot, but now you know too much."

"You know too much!"

A man dressed as Adolf Hitler visited a psychiatrist. "You can see I have no problems," he said. "I have the greatest army in the world, all the money I will ever need and every conceivable luxury you can imagine."

"Then what seems to be your problem?" asked the doctor.

"It's my wife," said the man. "She thinks she's a Mrs. Weaver."

* * *

Webster went to see a psychiatrist. "What's troubling you?" asked the doctor.

"Nothing," said Webster, "but my family thought I should come because I like cotton socks."

"Lots of people like cotton socks," said the headshrinker. "As a matter of fact, I like cotton socks myself."

"You do?" cried Webster. "How do you like yours, with oil and vinegar, or just a squeeze of lemon?"

While the child psychologist was studying some reports, his small daughter played with the girl who lived next door.

Suddenly, his daughter gave the girl a violent shove and stabbed her with a knife. Before the psychologist could stop her, his daughter turned to him and asked innocently, "Tell me, Daddy, why did I do that?"

* * *

Watkins, the psychiatrist, was giving Blair, his young patient, a series of tests. The shrink showed him a triangle and asked, "What's this?"

"A keyhole, and wow, look what's going on behind there!"

Dr. Watkins held up a rectangle, "And this?"

"A motel window, and boy, look what's going on behind there!" hinted Blair.

"And this?" he concluded, showing him a circle.

"A porthole, and oh my, look what's going on behind there!"

"Well," said the psychiatrist, "you certainly are sexually disturbed."

"*I'm* sexually disturbed! What about you . . . showing me all those dirty pictures!"

DEATH DILLIES

Jameson was on a train reading about birth and death statistics in the paper. Suddenly he turned to the woman next to him and said, "Do you know that every time I breathe a man dies?"

"Very interesting," she said. "Have you tried mouthwash?"

*　　*　　*

Sloan the faith healer ran into his old friend Thorpe and asked him how things were going.

"Not so good," was the pained reply. "My brother is very sick."

"Your brother isn't sick," contradicted the faith healer. "He only thinks he's sick. Remember that, he only thinks he's sick."

Two months later they met again and Sloan asked, "How's your brother now?"

"Worse," groaned Thorpe, "he thinks he's dead."

DRUG ADDICT'S DEFINITION
Death is the greatest kick of all
That's why they save it for last

* * *

Finkelstein was making his will. "Insert a clause," he instructed his lawyer, "to the effect that when I am dead I want all my relations to come and dance on my grave. Then bury me at sea."

* * *

Stafford went to the doctor for an examination. "You need more exercise," said the doctor.

"Nonsense," he said. "I get plenty of exercise acting as pallbearer for my friends who exercise."

* * *

Who is the meanest man in the world?

The warden who put a tack on the electric chair.

A big-time gambler had just died. The funeral drew a heavy crowd, mainly his professional friends. In eulogy, the minister said, "Tony is not dead. He only sleeps."

From the rear came a voice, "I got five grand says he don't wake up."

* * *

McMurray, age 86, was very ill. At his bedside Mrs. McMurray sat writing a letter.

Suddenly, the old man said, "I'm going to die, I know it."

"Nonsense," his wife assured him. "The doctor is optimistic you will get well."

Reassured, McMurray calmed down and his wife returned to her letter. "My dear," she asked suddenly, "do you spell 'crematory' with one 'r' or two?"

* * *

Chaplain (to condemned man in electric chair) : Can I do anything for you?
Prisoner: Yeah. Hold my hand.

Mrs. O'Reilly wasted little time on her man when he died and had him cremated. Immediately a salesman for gilded vases and enamel-crusted boxes descended upon her. "These containers are in very fine taste to hold the ashes," he said.

"It's no box he'll be in," she screamed. "I'm putting the ashes in an hourglass. All his life O'Reilly was a loafer, but now on the mantelpiece he'll be working all the time."

* * *

FAME
What you get for dying at the right time

* * *

There was a knock on the door. Mrs. Jennings opened it.

"Are you the widow Jennings?" asked a small boy.

"I'm Mrs. Jennings," she replied, "but I'm not a widow."

"Oh, no?" said the lad, "wait 'til you see who they're carrying upstairs."

There was a young Scottie named Dave
Who kept a dead whore in a cave
And when he was told
"You'll find her too cold!"
Said: "Think o' the money I save!"

* * *

McGregor on his deathbed told his wife he had left her his entire fortune of $25,-000.

"You're a good man," she sighed. "Have you any last wish?"

"Aye," said the Scotsman, "a wee plateful of that ham in the fridge."

"Oh, but you know you canna—that's for the mourners—after the funeral."

* * *

NOTICE IN FUNERAL PARLOR
Owing to the holidays this month we
shall be working with a skeleton staff

Rhoades fell out the window, head first. His widow collected in insurance, as well as the federal, state and Social Security benefits. But then came the lawyers, relatives, government deductions, bills, and inheritance tax. When the doctor came to see her, she was a nervous wreck.

"Sometimes," she cried, "I almost wish my husband hadn't fallen out the window."

* * *

Willis was crying as he knelt in front of the three tombstones lined up next to each other.

"Relatives of yours?" a passerby asked.

"This one is my first wife," he said. "She died from eating poisoned mushrooms. And this is my second wife. She also died from eating poisoned mushrooms.

"What about the third?" asked the stranger.

"Fractured skull."

"How come?"

"She wouldn't eat the poisoned mushrooms."

DEATH
*Nature's way of telling you to slow
down*

* * *

Mrs. Blair got a knock on the door.

"It's your husband!" shouted her neighbor, "He's face-down in the swimming pool. I think he's drowned."

"Is today Wednesday?" asked Mrs. Blair.

"Yes, it is, but ..."

"What time is it?"

"Eleven o'clock, but ..."

"Then don't worry about a thing," said Mrs. Blair. "The pool man will be here in an hour."

* * *

"When I die I want to be cremated," Kettner said.

"That would be just like you," replied his wife, "to go away and leave ashes lying all over the house."

Private Hadley's wife died suddenly while he was overseas, and his first sergeant was trying to figure out the best way to tell him. After much soul-searching, he decided to let Corporal Collins carry out the unpleasant task. "But break it to him gently," he told Collins.

The corporal went outside and called the men into formation. "Men," he said, "I want all of you who are married to take a step forward. . . . Uh, not so fast, Hadley."

* * *

A widow consulted a medium, who put her into communication with her late husband.

"Howard," said the woman, "are you happy now?"

"I am very happy," replied the spirit.

"Are you happier than you were on the earth with me?"

"Yes, I am far happier than I was on earth with you."

"What is it like in heaven?"

"Heaven!" exclaimed Howard. "I'm not in heaven!"

The two skeletons in the corner closet were grumbling about the heat, the dust, the boredom.

"What are we staying here for anyhow?" one asked.

"Damned if I know," the second skeleton answered. "I'd leave in a minute if I had any guts."

"I'd leave in a minute if I had any
guts."

The death angel smote Demetrius Per-
due
  And gave him protracted repose;
  He wore a checked shirt and a number
twelve shoe,
  And he had a huge wart on his nose.
  No doubt he is happier dwelling in
space
  Over there on the evergreen shore.
  His friends are informed that his fu-
neral takes place
  Precisely at quarter past four.

* * *

Governor Wallace was sitting in a doctor's office. "I've got bad news and worst
news for you," said the M.D.

"What's the bad news?" said Wallace.

"The bad news is you've got an incura-
ble disease."

"Oh, God! What could be worse?"

"You've got sickle cell anemia," said the
doctor.

New York City was jammed for the convention. Every hotel and rooming house was full. Phillip was tired. He simply had to find a place to sleep that night.

"Anything will do," he said to the hotel clerk.

"I can let you have a cot in the ballroom," replied the clerk, "but there's a woman in the opposite corner. If you don't make any noise she'll be none the wiser."

"Fine," said Phillips. He went to the ballroom but five minutes later came running out to the clerk.

"Say," he cried, "that woman in there is dead!"

"I know," was the answer, "but how did you find out?"

*   *   *

Did you hear about the guy whose nostril hairs were so long, one day he sneezed and flogged himself to death?

*   *   *

And then there was the judge who told the condemned man, "You'll die when you hear this one."

Attorney Gross was cross-examining the defendant.

"After you poisoned the coffee, your husband sat at the breakfast table with you and sipped it. Didn't you feel the slightest pity for him?"

"Yes," she answered. "There was just one moment when I felt sorry for him."

"When was that?" inquired the lawyer.

"When he asked for a second cup."

* * *

REPOSE IN RHYME

Oh! Bury Little Bernard out in the woods,
In a beautiful hole in the ground,
Where the bumblebees buzz and the woodpeckers sing,
And the straddlebugs tumble around;
So that, in winter, when the snow and the slush
Have covered his last little bed,
His brother Nathaniel can go out with Ann
And visit the place with his sled.

114

An M.D. in Boston looked down at the meanest man in the world. "You're dying, Frank. Are you willing to go?"

"Yes," piped Frank weakly.

"Well, that helps," murmured the medico. "For now that makes it unanimous."

* * *

Nelson was very sentimental. "Today is a very important anniversary," he told his son. "William Tell was born 900 years ago today. When I was a kid, William Tell was my idol. I remember I used to go in the backyard with my best friend. He would put an apple on his head and I would shoot it off. He would have been thirty-four tomorrow...."

It was Schneider's birthday, and that morning there was a knock on the door. "Telegram!"

Schneider opened the door excitedly. "Is it a singing telegram?" he asked the messenger boy.

"No, sir. We don't have singing telegrams anymore."

"I've always wanted a singing telegram. Can't you bend the rules and make an old man happy?"

"Sorry."

"Please," begged Schneider. "Today's my birthday."

"Oh, all right," said the boy, "Dah-dah dah dah-dah-dah . . . your sister Rose is dead!"

* * *

FUNERAL FUNNIES

"All this talk about back-seat drivers is overrated. I've been driving for twenty years and I've never heard a word from behind."

"What sort of car do you drive?"

"A hearse."

*　　*　　*

Henderson called the local funeral director and asked, "Would you please come up right away? I want you to supervise my wife's funeral."

"But that's impossible, Mr. Henderson," said the undertaker, "I buried your wife three years ago."

"Yes, but I remarried."

"Well," replied the mortician, "Congratulations!"

The son was sitting at the bedside of the elderly gentleman who was dying. "Where do you want to be buried," the kid asked, "in Forest Lawn or Hillside Memorial Park?"

The old man creaked up on his elbow and answered, "Surprise me!"

*　*　*

SIGN IN A FUNERAL PARLOR
WE GIVE GREEN STAMPS

*　*　*

"Daddy, can my new boyfriend replace your business partner who died this morning?"

"It's OK with me, if you can arrange it with the undertaker."

*　*　*

Did you hear about the undertaker who married a snake charmer?

They had towels marked "Hiss" and "Hearse."

118

Down the street his funeral goes,
  As sobs and wails diminish;
He died from drinking straight shellac,
  But he had a lovely finish.

* * *

A funeral procession was winding its way to the cemetery. The business partner of the deceased was following behind the hearse until, just before they reached their destination, a big coal truck pulled out from a side road into an opening between the hearse and the first car.

Upon seeing the coal truck ahead of him, the partner remarked, "I know where Norman's going, but I didn't think he had to supply his own fuel."

* * *

During funeral services for old Mr. Eckerman, the undertaker sidled up to Mrs. Eckerman and inquired, "How old a man was your husband?"

"Ninety-eight," replied his widow. "Two years older than I."

"My, my," replied the mortician, "hardly worth going home, is it?"

119

Did you hear about the opportunistic mortician who ran a combination mortuary and get well card shop?

* * *

Watson read his name in the obituary column. He immediately called up his friend, "Hey, Jim, did you read my name in the obituary column?"

"Yeah," Jim replied. "Where are you calling from?"

* * *

Bob, Steve and Rick were walking in a cemetery. "When you die who would you like to be placed alongside of?" asked Rick of his buddies.

"Abe Lincoln," said Bob.

"George Washington," said Steve.

"Well," said Rick, "I'd like to be next to Raquel Welch."

"Wait a minute," said Steve. "She ain't dead yet."

"I know," said Rick, "but neither am I."

SIGN IN FUNERAL PARLOR
WE'LL BE THE LAST ONES TO LET YOU DOWN

* * *

Mrs. Fowler's husband was laid out in a funeral parlor.

Suddenly, she decided she didn't like the brown suit her husband had on.

Mrs. Fowler found the funeral director and said, "I see another man wearing a blue suit in the next parlor. Blue was my husband's favorite color and I'd like him laid out in a blue suit."

The director was happy to comply, and told the woman to return in half an hour and the change would be made.

Mrs. Fowler returned in five minutes and happily found her husband now lying in a blue suit, the other one in a brown suit.

"How did you change the suits so fast?" she asked the undertaker.

"I didn't change suits," he replied. "I found it was easier to just switch heads."

The hearse rounded the corner at sixty miles an hour. Suddenly, the back door opened up and the casket slid out, banged into the curb and landed on the sidewalk at the feet of a wino. Spreading out his arms, the drunk yelled, "Safe!"

"My uncle's got a weird job."

"What's that?"

"Interior decorator for coffins."

*   *   *

Did you hear about the mortician who's going crazy because every morning his wife comes down to the mortuary and rearranges the coffins?

*   *   *

His wife lay on her deathbed.

"Fred," she pleaded, "I want you to promise me that you'll ride in the same car with Mother at my funeral."

"OK," sighed the husband, "but it's going to ruin my whole day."

The actor died and played to standing room only at his funeral. His agent said to a friend, "If he knew he would have an audience like this, he would have died years ago."

*　　*　　*

Where else but Southern California could this happen? The *Los Angeles Times* advertised a cemetery for people who believe in reincarnation. It includes kitchen privileges.

*　　*　　*

SIGN IN A FUNERAL PARLOR
MUST YOU BE GOING? TRY US

*　　*　　*

Harrigan: At my funeral I want you to pour a bottle of Irish whiskey over my grave.
Calihan: Sure, but would you mind if I passed it through me kidneys first?

The Toastmaster General George Jessel very often doubles at two eulogies in one day. He is proud that he is known as a great funeral orator. Once, at a particularly tender moment during his eulogy, he accidentally glanced down on the deceased in the coffin. "My God," Jessel gasped, "I *know* this man."

"I *know* this man."

Something had gone wrong at the crematorium. The manager looked out his window and saw a queue of hearses all up the drive. He rushed out and said to his foreman: "What the blazes is the hold up?"

"Sorry, boss, but we've got a coffin stuck, it won't go in the oven."

The manager rushed to have a look, and to his amazement, he saw that it was a Y-shaped coffin. He ran back to the office, rang up the undertaker, and said: "What the hell'd you mean by sending me a Y-shaped coffin?"

"I couldn't help it, I had no choice," said the undertaker.

"What do you mean, you couldn't help it?"

"She was a very sexy young woman."

*　　*　　*

Whose funeral parlor does he use when an undertaker buries another undertaker?

"My grandpa was a very clean person. He took ten showers a day."

"But he died yesterday, didn't he?"

"Yeah, and in tribute to him the whole funeral procession went through a car wash."

*   *   *

Since many complaints have been filed against the high cost of burials, a San Francisco funeral parlor has offered a solution. They have a budget funeral where they don't engrave the headstone. They cut the deceased's name out of the phone book and just paste it on.

And if you can't afford that, they just wrap you up in a big plastic bag, set you down at the airport and let somebody steal you.

*   *   *

Mort Fleischmann, RCA's lovable West Coast public information director, says, "On 14th Street, in New York, where I grew up, the neighborhood was so dangerous the mortician drove a double decker hearse."

"Was it cold down at the mortuary?"

"You kiddin'? Three corpses had goose bumps so big they had to let out their coffins."

*　　*　　*

"Haywood the undertaker is doing some big business!"

"Why not? Look at the terrific location he's got—right next to the doctor's office."

*　　*　　*

Friend at a funeral: It must be hard to lose a wife.
Bereaved: Almost impossible.

*　　*　　*

Mrs. Eckert was watching a new production of "Fiddler on the Roof." Suddenly, a man approached her and asked, "Pardon me, madam, but do you mind if I occupy that empty seat next to you?"

"Not at all," she replied. "I expected it to be taken when I bought the tickets, but all my friends are at my husband's funeral."

Ed Bluestone, one of the best of the new comedians, has developed a plan for funerals of people he didn't like:

Pass out baby pictures of the deceased.

Shake the widow's hand with an electric buzzer.

Stand around the cemetery saying, "At least he'll no longer be tormented over being impotent."

Tell the clergyman that the deceased was a vampire and ask if you can drive a stake through his heart.

Show up at the cemetery masquerading as the deceased.

On the way home from the cemetery, tell the widow that you think you saw the body move.

The day after the funeral, send the widow a candygram from the deceased.

* * *

Did you hear about the ambitious mortician who kept bringing his work home with him?

Walter watched anxiously at his wife's bedside during her illness. "You look so peaked," she said, "why don't you go out and take a walk?"

He came back in an hour, full of news. "Say you know who just got engaged?" he asked.

The dying woman opened her eyes and asked, "Who?"

"Me!"

* * *

Stanfield met a famous actor after his wife's funeral. "God," said Stanfield, "you certainly made a spectacle of yourself at the church, falling in a faint and dragging the corpse out of the coffin, and kissing her that way!"

"That was nothing—you should have caught my act at the grave."

* * *

FUNERAL FUN

A silly young fellow named Hyde,
In a funeral procession was spied,
When asked, "Who is dead?"
He giggled and said,
"I don't know; I just came for the ride."

Fineberg the funeral director was lunching with his friend Weinstein. "I got a good bargain for you in a coffin."

"I don't like to think about things like that. How much?"

"It's made of mahogany with silver handles and a lock. For you $2,000."

"I'll think about it."

On his way home from work, Weinstein stopped at the Minkis Mortuary to compare prices. "I can give you something nice," said the director. "I've got a mahogany coffin, with silver handles and I'll even throw in a lock. The price is $1,000."

Weinstein rushed over to Fineberg's and began screaming, "Some friend you are. I just saw the same coffin you wanted to sell me and it was a thousand dollars cheaper."

"Was it mahogany, with silver handles and a lock."

"Yes," replied Weinstein.

"Did it have a silk lining?"

"I didn't look. I don't think so."

"You see!" said Fineberg. "In six months you'll need a new lining."

* * *

GRAVE GIGGLES

Here are some epitaphs from gravesites around the world:

BOSTON, MASS.

Here under this sod and under these trees
Is buried the body of Solomon Pease,
But here in this hole lies only his pod
His soul is shelled out and gone to God.

* * *

YORKSHIRE, ENG.

Here lies my wife, a sad slattern and
*   shrew;*
If I said I regretted her, I should lie too!

PARIS, FR.
(translated)
Here lies Louis Fouchard, grocer.

*His inconsolable widow dedicates this
 monument*

*to his memory, and continues the same
 business at*

the old stand, 273 Rue Fontainebleau

*   *   *

DANBURY, CONN.
Here lies my husbands, I, II, III,
Dumb as men could ever be.
As for my IV'th, well, praise be God!
He bides for a little above the sod.
*Alex, Ben, Sandy were the first three's
 names,*
*And to make things tidy, I'll add his
 James.*

*   *   *

INTERCOURSE, PENN.
Here lies Agatha, Brunner's wife,
She lived six years in calm and strife.
Death came at last and set her free,
I was glad and so was she.

EUGENE, ORE.

Here Betsy Brown her body, lies,
Her soul is flying to the skies.
While here on earth she oft-times spun
Six hundred skeins from sun to sun,
And wove one day, her daughter brags,
Two hundred pounds of carpet rags.

*　　*　　*

CANTON, OHIO

He heard the angels calling him
From the Celestial Shore,
He flapped his wings and away he went
To make one angel more.

*　　*　　*

FORT WAYNE, IND.

Beneath these stones do lie,
Back to back, my wife and I!
When the last trumpet the air shall fill,
If she gets up, I'll just lie still.

MORRISTOWN, N.J.

Here lies a man who was killed by light-
ning;
He died when his prospects seemed to be
brightening,
He might have cut a flash in this world of
trouble,
But the flash cut him, and he lies in the
stubble.

* * *

LYNCHBURG, VA.

This stone was raised by Tillie's lord,
Not Tillie's virtues to record—
For they're well known to all the town—
But it was raised to keep her down.

* * *

FARGO, N.D.

Here lies my wife: here let her lie!
Now she's at rest—and so am I.

MANCHESTER, VT.

Beneath this stone, a lump of clay, lies A'rabella Young;
Who on the 21st of May began to hold her tongue.

* * *

SAN ANTONIO, TEX.

Here lie I and my two daughters,
Killed by drinking Mexican waters.
If we had stuck to Epsom Salts
We wouldn't be lying in these vaults.

* * *

ROCHESTER, N.Y.

Here lies, cut down like unripe fruit,
The wife of Pastor David Root
She died of drinking too much coffee,
Anno Domini eighteen forty.

* * *

SPRINGFIELD, MISS.

Underneath this pile of stones
Lies all that's left of Milly Jones.
Her name was Boyd, it was not Jones,
But Jones was used to rhyme with stones!

SACRED TO THE MEMORY
OF MORTIMER BIXBY
WHO DIED SEPT. 12, 1884

HIS WIDOW, AGED 24,
LIVES AT 7 ELM STREET,
HAS EVERY QUALIFICATION
FOR A GOOD WIFE, AND YEARNS
TO BE COMFORTED.

BROADWAY, ENG.

Here lies the body of Richard Bleven
Killed by lightning sent from heaven
For trading horses on Sunday, June eleven,
In the year Eighteen Hundred Twenty-
seven.

* * *

BANGOR, ME.

Open wide ye heavenly gates
That lead to the heavenly shore;
Our father suffered in passing through
And Mother weighs much more.

* * *

NORTH PLATTE, NEB.

Here lies the bones of Daniel Fourton
Whose death, alas! was strangely brought
on.
Trying his corns one day to mow off,
His razor slipped and cut his toe off.
His toe, or, rather, what it grew to,
An inflammation quickly flew to.
Which took, alas! to mortifying
And was the cause of Daniel's dying.

140

BATON ROUGE, LA.

Beneath this stone our baby lays,
He neither cries nor hollers,
He lived just one and twenty days,
And cost us forty dollars.

* * *

KILKENNY, IRE.

Neuralgia worked on Mrs. Dent,
Till 'neath the sod it laid her.
She was a worthy Protestant
And served as a crusader.

* * *

PEORIA, ILL.

Here lies Poor Charlotte,
Who died no harlot,
But in her virginity,
Though just turned nineteen
Which within this vicinity
Is hard to be found and seen.

LARAMIE, WY.

Here lies the clay of Mitchel Coots,
Whose feet yet occupy his boots.
His soul has gone—we know not where
It landed, neither do we care.
He slipped a joker up his sleeve
With vile intention to deceive;
And when detected, tried to jerk
His gun, but didn't get his work
In with sufficient swiftness, which
Explains the presence here of Mitch.

* * *

WAUSAW, WIS.

At rest beneath this slab of stone,
Lies stingy Joseph Wyett;
He died one morning just at ten
And saved a dinner by it!

* * *

CONCORD, N.H.

Here lies the body of Rick Eldred,
At least, he will be when he's dead;
But now at this time he's alive,
The 18 of July sixty-five.

HARRISBURG, PA.

In memory of our father: Gone to join his appendix, his tonsils, his olfactory nerve, his kidney, his eardrum, and a leg prematurely removed by an interne who craved the experience.

* * *

LITTLE ROCK, ARK.

Here lieth Matthew Hollingshead
Who died from cold caught in his head.
It brought on fever and rheumatiz,
Which ended me—for here I is!

* * *

GRAND RAPIDS, MICH.

Here lies Ann Mann;
She lived an old Maid and died an old
Mann

FAIRBANKS, ALASKA

Beneath this stone, a lump of clay,
Lies Uncle Peter Dan'els
Who too early in the month of May
Took off his winter flannels!

* * *

FROM A BOOT HILL CEMETERY IN DODGE CITY, KANS.

Here lies
Lester Moore
Four slugs
From a .44
No Les
No More

* * *

BOOT HILL, PECOS, TX.

Played five aces.
Now playing the harp.

Maynard was a rough man to do business with. He always insisted on dating his checks ahead. When he finally died, his tombstone read, "Here lies Earl Maynard, died March 8 as of April 15."

* * *

Remember, friend, as you pass by,
As you are now, so once was I.
As I am now, thus you shall be,
So be prepared to follow me.

* * *

Here lies till Gabriel's trumpet peal
The bones of Sheldon Sharp.
He dozed while holding a steering wheel
And woke up holding a harp.

Here rests poor Mrs. Ben Mummers,
Her weary heart sprung a bad leak
When her daughter of sixteen summers
Stayed home every night for a week.

* * *

The children of Israel wanted bread
And the Lord sent them manna,
Old clerk Wallace wanted a wife
And the Devil sent him Anna.

* * *

Here lies my wife beneath
The ornate coffin lid.
Still able to make love.
As well as she ever did.

* * *

Here lies the father of twenty-nine.
He would have had more
    but he didn't have time.

Tom's pushing up daisies now
With his toes
Raced a train to a crossing,
Lost by a nose.

* * *

Joe tried to cross the railroad track
Before a passing train;
They put the pieces in a sack;
But couldn't find his brain.

* * *

He was always a polite man. Even his tombstone read, "Pardon me for not rising."

* * *

These epitaphs were discovered on the tombstones of:

A HYPOCHONDRIAC
I told you I was sick

A DENTIST
Stranger! Approach this spot with gravity!
Lou Kane is filling his last cavity

* * *

A PEDESTRIAN
This is the grave of Mike O'Day
Who died maintaining his right of way.
His right was clear, his will was strong,
But he's just as dead as if he'd been wrong.

* * *

A FISHERMAN
Here lies the body of Jonathan Stout,
He fell in the water and never got out,
And still is supposed to be floating about.

* * *

AN ORATOR
Here lies the body of Cynthia Near
Whose mouth it stretched from ear to ear.
Tread softly, stranger, o'er this wonder,
For if she yawns, you're gone by thunder!

148

AN OLD MAID
Who says you can't take it with you?

*　＊　　＊　　＊*

A WAITER
God finally caught his eye

*　＊　　＊　　＊*

AN ATTORNEY
Here lies a lawyer and an honest man.
Who ever thought there'd be room for two
*　men in one little grave?*

*　＊　　＊　　＊*

A PLUMBER
Here lies a good plumber, James Neville,
Whose head was as straight as his level.
*　We have laid him to rest,*
*　On his face, pointing west,*
And his sex life has gone to the devil.

A MARBLE CUTTER NAMED
RUPERT SCOTT
Here lies Mary Alice
Wife of Rupert Scott, Marble Cutter

This monument was erected by Rupert Scott as a tribute to her memory and a specimen of his artistic skill in the manufacture of tombstones. Monuments of this size and style are three hundred dollars, payment on completion of the work.

* * *

A MISER
Here lies one for medicine would not give
A little gold, and so his life he lost;
I fancy now he'd wish to live again,
Could he but know how much his funeral
cost.

* * *

A TEACHER
School is out
Teacher has gone home

A FIREMAN

William P. Monroe,
Died 1878, aged 38;
He has answered
His last alarm.

* * *

And then we have the Texas undertaker
who carves the following on the bottom of
all his monuments:

    Ashes to ashes, dust to dust
We bury only the upper crust
    McConnell Funeral Home

* * *

Here are a few inscriptions—fictitious,
of course—that might fittingly adorn the
gravestones of some famous personalities:

CLIVE BROOK

Excuse me for not rising

LIONEL BARRYMORE

Well, I've played everything but a
harp

WALTER WINCHELL
*Here lies Walter Winchell in the dirt
he loved so well*

ILKA CHASE
*I've finally gotten to the bottom of
things*

DOROTHY PARKER
Involved in a plot

ROBERT BENCHLEY
This is all over my head

GEORGE BERNARD SHAW
*I knew if I stayed long enough
something like this would happen*

DOCTOR ALBERT SCHWEITZER
*If cannibals should ever catch me
I hope they will say:
"We have eaten Doctor Schweitzer
And he was good to the end . . .
And the end wasn't bad."*

BOB BURNS
Will you please get your damn
feet off me—I want to turn over!

EDDIE CANTOR
Here in nature's arms I nestle
Free at last from Georgie Jessel

JOE E. LEWIS
If I had my life to live over again
I wouldn't have the strength to do it

WILL ROGERS
Here lies Will Rogers.
Politician turned honest—and he
starved to death

W.C. FIELDS
On the whole I'd rather be in Philadelphia

JOHNNY CARSON
I'll be right back!

* * *

CRAZY COMICS

During the colorful nightclub era comedians were forced to cope with a new kind of audience. Previously, they had performed in vaudeville and burlesque theatres, where people sat facing the stage and were mostly polite.

Night spots and cafes presented a different atmosphere. People clumped together at tables where both food and drinks were served. And often, the booze-brave patrons attempted to disconcert the comics by heckling them.

The gagsters, forced to defend themselves, came up with Heckler Savers, *jokes that would put the heckler in his place and at the same time evoke laughter from the rest of the crowd. In time, "putting down the audience" became an art and eventually led to the popularity of funnymen like Fat Jack Leonard and Don Rickles.*

The following "squelchers" used by nightclub comics have become classics. You'll notice, they also happen to be sick:

Is that your beard or do you have a hairy tongue?

I'll buy you a funeral plot if you move right in.

Did your mother have any children that lived?

Didn't I see you in a bottle of alcohol?

Didn't I see your face on a bottle of iodine?

Why don't you take a powder—like arsenic?

Why don't you throw your hat away and keep your head in it?

Why don't you touch a live wire with wet hands?

Why don't you visit a near-sighted knife thrower?

Why don't you take a bath in quicksand?

Why don't you take a bath in a cement mixer?

Why don't you take a nap on a railroad track?

Why don't you step in front of a moving steam roller and iron your brain?

Why don't you stick some dynamite into your ears and blow your brains apart?

You look like a self-made nobody.

You look like a side dish nobody ordered.

You look like an unmade bed.

You look like the first husband of a widow.

You look like you're walking around just to save funeral expenses.

You look like an accident waiting to happen.

You look like a canceled stamp.

You look like a dead-end street.

You look like a detour on the road of life.

You look like a floorwaker in a junk yard.

You look like a freckle on the nose of time.

You look like a human being, but looks can be deceiving.

You look like a man who got sick during the voyage of his life.

* * *

Most comedians delight in using a joke known as the one-liner, so called because the point of the gag can be expressed in one sentence or one line. Here are some of the best:

"Other than that, Mrs. Lincoln, how did you like the play?"

"Mrs. Custer, would you like to contribute to Indian relief?"

"Happy Father's Day, Mr. Lindbergh."

"Did your husband get his polio shots yet, Mrs. Roosevelt?"

"Mrs. Dean, has Jimmy got his car fixed yet?"

"You're about as funny as a carload of dead babies."

"I don't care what your reason is, Mrs. Lincoln, I still say no ticket refunds."

"You're about as funny as a mouthful of cancer."

"There is a bus leaving in ten minutes. Be under it."

"Here's your cigar back. I heard your baby died."

"Grandmother! Use the bottle opener. You'll ruin your gums."

"I don't care if your name is Santa Claus. Get your hand out of my stocking."

"I don't care if your name is Napoleon. Get your hand out of my blouse."

"I don't care who you are, fat man. Get your reindeer off my roof."

"To my nephew Charlie, who always said I'd never remember him in my will . . . hello, Charlie."

"I don't care who you are. Get that cross off my hill."

"Go home, Mary. I'll be here for quite a while."

"I'm going to take you out of the parade if you don't stop dragging your cross."

"I don't care what star you are following. Get your darn camel off my lawn."

"There won't be any Easter this year—they found the body."

*　*　*

"I don't care who you are. Don't walk on the water while I'm fishing."

"It was the night before Xmas and Mary fell off the donkey."

"I don't care who the kid is. Get him out of my manger."

"I don't care what supper this is, there will be no drinks served at this table."

"I don't care if this is the Last Supper. You can't serve wine without a liquor license."

"I don't care if this is the Last Supper. It's $2.50 a plate."

George Carlin, the collegians' favorite comedian, kills audiences with these sickies from his News of the Day *routine:*

"I'd like to take a look at the news. First of all the headlines: The government has just announced that saliva causes cancer . . . but only when swallowed in small amounts."

A woman was severely injured today when she attempted to force feed a wildcat.

A dog exploded on a busy downtown street corner today. No one was killed, however 12 people were overcome by fur.

Police estimate also that 50 to 60 fleas also lost their lives in the blast.

A man, 65 years old, James Driscoll, was asleep in his downtown hotel room last Wednesday, when he was awakened by the sound of a dog barking. When he woke he found the room was full of smoke; he could not see and the dog led him out of the room, down the hall, and into an elevator shaft where he plunged eight stories.

Out at the lake at City Park today, police arrested a one-armed man who was bothering the other boaters by continuously rowing in a circle.

And here are a few sickie favorites from some other funnymen:

"Live each day as if it is your last," Fred Allen once said, "and one of these days you'll be right."

Phyllis Diller asks, "How can you tell a widow in Beverly Hills?

"She's the one wearing the black tennis clothes."

Rodney Dangerfield says, "When I was young, the kids called me 'four-eyes.' Then I got glasses, and they called me 'eight-eyes.' "

George Gobel was asked to come up with a slogan over the July 4 weekend to encourage safe driving. George suggested:

"Ladies and gentlemen, this is a holiday weekend. The National Safety Council estimates that 524 people will be killed nationwide. So far only 185 have been killed. Some of you folks aren't trying."

*   *   *

CANNIBAL CACKLES

A cannibal rushed into his village to spread the word that a hunting party had captured a politician.

"Good," said one of the cannibals, "I've always wanted to try a baloney sandwich."

* * *

Cannibal Chief to Victim: What did you do for a living?

Victim: I was an associate editor.

Cannibal: Cheer up. After tonight you'll be editor-in-chief.

Each day the natives would cut the missionary's arm and suck his blood. Finally, "Kill me if you want, but I'm sick and tired of getting stuck for the drinks."

* * *

CANNIBAL COOKBOOK
How To Serve Your Fellow Man

* * *

One day in the jungle an explorer came upon some cannibals who were just about to eat a meal. The head of the tribe confided to the white man that he had been educated in Britain and had been to Oxford.

"Do you mean to say," asked the explorer, "that you went to a university and yet you still eat your enemies?"

"Oh, yes," was the reply. "But now I use a knife and fork."

Little Girl Cannibal: Mommy, is that airplane up there good to eat?
Mamma Cannibal: Just like a lobster, dear. Only what's inside.

* * *

A cannibal chief was traveling to New York to speak on behalf of his tribe at the United Nations. He entered the dining room of the ocean liner and was seated by a steward who asked, "Would you like to see a menu?"

"No," said the chief, "just bring me the passenger list."

* * *

First Cannibal: Am I late for dinner?
Second Cannibal: Yes, everybody's eaten.

Two cannibals met in a mental institution. One was tearing out pictures of men, women and children from a magazine, stuffing them into his mouth and eating them.

"Tell me," said the other, "is that dehydrated stuff really any good?"

* * *

Mamma Cannibal to Witch Doctor: I'm worried about Junior. He wants to be a vegetarian.

* * *

An African tribe was having a terrible time with its crops. The natives went to the chief, who said, "Let's send a telegram to the Russians telling them we are having agricultural problems and need their assistance. They'll send us seeds and tractors and one hundred young technicians to help us. Then we'll send a telegram to the Americans telling them that the Russians are helping us, and the Americans will send us seeds and tractors and one hundred technicians. When all the technicians arrive, we'll eat them."

An American hunter stopped at an isolated bar in the interior of Africa. As he lounged at the bar downing a strong native brew, in walked a tiny man about one foot high immaculately dressed in a British army uniform.

Noticing the tourist staring openmouthed at the diminutive newcomer, the bartender remarked, "I see you haven't met the Major before. Speak up, Major. Tell the Yank about the time you called the witch doctor a bloody fake."

"Speak up, Major!"

Cannibal to witch doctor: "Hey, Doc, something is wrong with my kid. He won't eat anybody."

*   *   *

What do cannibals eat when they go on a diet?
Pygmies.

*   *   *

What did the cannibal have for supper?
Baked beings on toast.

*   *   *

What do cannibals play at parties?
"Swallow My Leader."

*   *   *

There was a young cannibal called Ned
Who used to eat onions in bed.
  His mother said, "Sonny,
  It's not very funny,
Why don't you eat people instead?"

CANNIBAL
One who is fed up with people

* * *

A missionary, lost in the jungle, was beset by a lion. The missionary knelt in prayer, then looked up to see the lion on his knees, too.

"Brother," said the relieved missionary, "how delightful it is to join you in prayer when I feared you were going to eat me."

"Don't interrupt," said the lion, "I'm saying grace."

* * *

"Well," said the missionary to his colleague, speaking from inside the cannibal's pot, "at least this will be their first taste of religion."

The hunter was captured by the African tribe. Just as they were about to boil him in soupgreens, he exclaimed, "Look here. I make fire!" With that, he flicked his lighter and it burst into flame. The cannibals fell back in amazement.

"Magic!" cried the hunter in triumph.

"It sure is," the chief replied. "It's the first time I ever saw a lighter work the first shot."

"First time I ever saw one work the first try!"

If a missionary is supposed to go to heaven and a cannibal is destined for hell, what happens when a cannibal dies after making a meal of a missionary?

* * *

"I hate my mother-in-law," one cannibal said to the other.
"Then just eat the noodles."

* * *

CANNIBAL THEME SONG
Just Give Me Something To Dismember You By

* * *

Did you hear about the cannibal who ate his mother-in-law and found out she still disagreed with him?

* * *

The young cannibal chief noticed a particularly beautiful young lady about to be placed in the kettle. "Wait," he shouted to the chef, "I'll have my breakfast in bed."

First Cannibal: Have you seen the dentist?

Second Cannibal: Yes. He filled my teeth at dinner.

* * *

"Shall I stew both those cooks we captured?" the cannibal cook asked his king.

"No," replied the king, "one is enough. Too many cooks spoil the broth."

* * *

Did you hear about the enterprising man seen at the crematorium gathering up ashes?

He sends them to cannibals so they can have instant people.

* * *

An explorer who had just returned from an African safari was describing his adventures before a room full of women.

"I suddenly came upon a tribe of wild women who had no tongues."

"No tongues? How in the world could they talk?"

"They couldn't," he explained. "That's what made them so wild."

179

Kirshbaum thought the cannibals would let him leave the jungle if he brought bananas as a gift for the cannibal chief. But they grabbed him and started stuffing them up his bottom. Brucker began howling with laughter.

"Why you laugh?" asked the chief.

"My friend is coming with pineapples!"

*　　*　　*

Mother Cannibal: How many times have I told you not to talk with someone in your mouth?

*　　*　　*

What would a cannibal be who ate his mother's sister?

An aunt-eater.

*　　*　　*

The chief asked the U.S. State Department to send him, in cultural exchange, a comic who tells dirty stories. He wanted to have some spiced ham for dinner.

As one teenage cannibal said to his date: "Let's take a stroll down to the old campfire and see who's cooking."

* * *

The chief's wife sent a message to another tribal chief in the neighborhood— "Please come and visit Saturday night— we're having the Browns for dinner."

* * *

AFRICAN LULLABY
She Was Only a Cannibal's Daughter
but
She Liked Her Men Stewed

In Africa, a white trader sat in his hut holding two pistols and playing classical records on his battery phonograph. He called his native boy, kicked him in the balls, and sent him to get a 12-year-old virgin. After raping the girl, both front and back, he shot her, and put another record on the phonograph.

"Here!" he shouted to the native boy, "drag the body away and get me another." As he raped the second little black girl, he heard native drums start beating: "Boom boom boom! Boom boom boom."

"What are those drums?" he shouted, taking a shot of heroin with a hypodermic needle in his upper thigh. "I can't stand those damn drums! Bring me the chief."

The chief was brought; he shot him instantly, and kicked the body down the stairs. Immediately the drums began again, "Boom boom boom! Boom boom boom! BOOM BOOM BOOM BOOM!!"

"What are those drums?" he shouted smashing all his records on the floor.

"They're mourning for the chief you just shot," said the native boy.

"Oh, my god, I can't *stand* it!" shouted the white man. "What time is it, anyhow?"

"It's midnight, Dr. Schweitzer."

*　　*　　*

SICK SICKIES

"Got a cigarette?"

"Here. Take the pack."

"Thanks. Got a match?"

"Here. You can keep this lighter."

"Thanks again. Say, have you got an oil well or something?"

"No. Lung cancer."

* * *

"I'm wondering ..."

"About what?"

"About a fellow I know. He was in an accident and lost both hands."

"Well, what are you wondering about?"

"I wonder how he feels."

The foreman of the lumber camp put Novack, a new workman, on the circular saw. As he turned away, he heard the man say, "Ouch."

"What happened?"

"Dunno," replied the Polack. "I just stuck out my hand like this, and . . . well, I'll be damned. There goes another one!"

* * *

WORLD'S SICKEST MOVIE
Chain-Saw Vasectomy

* * *

"What do you mean your wooden leg hurts you? You can't feel pain in a wooden leg."

"You don't understand. During the fight with this man—he hit me over the head with it."

* * *

The magician was describing his act to a booking agent. "I've got a new trick that will panic them," he declared, "I saw a woman in half."

"A new trick?" said the agent. "Magicians have been sawing women in half for years."

"Lengthwise?" said the prestidigitator.

184

Dunbar and Hunt, two Hollywood film producers, were making a war epic and decided to use armies of extras for the battle scenes, five thousand men on one side and four thousand on the other.

"That's colossal," said Dunbar, "but when the shooting is finished, we have to pay 9,000 extras. What do we do about that?"

"Simple," answered Hunt. "In the last battle we use real bullets."

* * *

Then there was the vampire actress who was waiting for a character she could really sink her teeth into.

* * *

"Patience, my ass," one vulture said to the other. "I'm gonna kill something."

* * *

The vulture had a sick expression on his face.

"What's wrong?" asked his wife.

"I think I ate something fresh."

Bleeker got into a taxi and said, "Hey, cabbie, do you have room in the front seat for three pizzas, two submarine sandwiches and a case of beer?"

"Sure."

"*Baaarf!!!*"

Sully was telling of his days as a salesman.

"Yeah," he said, "I sold a bottle of my miracle rub to a cripple. He rubbed some on his right leg and threw away his right crutch. Then he rubbed some on his left leg and threw away his left crutch."

"Well, what happened then?" asked his listener.

"Hell, he fell flat on his face. He couldn't walk without his crutches."

* * *

SCRAWLED ON BOSTON SUBWAY
*Hire the Handicapped. They're Fun To
Watch*

* * *

Two cockroaches were lunching in a nearby sewer. One of them was reporting on the new restaurant in the neighborhood.

"From all accounts the refrigerator is spotlessly white, the floor sparkles like polished platinum, there isn't a crack in the walls, and the ceiling is resplendent in chrome. And, mind you, not a speck of dirt in the place."

"Please, please," said the other roach, "not while I'm eating."

Fenton strolled into a department store and found the gift counselor, a young feminist.

"Could you suggest a gift for my aunt?" asked the man. "She's in her late eighties, and she's very wealthy."

"What about some floor wax," cracked the girl.

*　*　*

MACHO
Jogging home from your own vasectomy

*　*　*

Captain Kilby and the crew of his ship-wrecked vessel had been in a life-boat for ten days and had nothing left to eat. The captain offered to kill himself so that the men could eat his body. As he lifted a revolver to his temple, one of the men shouted, "Stop, Captain, stop!"

His face ashen, Captain Kilby let the muzzle of the revolver fall. "Yes?" he asked.

"Don't shoot yourself in the head, Captain," pleaded the sailor, "brains are my favorite dish."

Ralph wrangled a date with Marianne, a gorgeous model who lived in the penthouse apartment of a 36-floor building on Park Avenue.

"Look, I'll be a little late," she phoned him. "The doorman will let you in. Just make yourself comfortable and play with Duke."

Ralph got to the penthouse suite and Duke turned out to be a huge Great Dane who insisted on fetching a tennis ball. Ralph threw it into the bedroom, the dog returned it. He tossed it into the kitchen, the Great Dane brought it back. He threw the ball out on to the balcony. The ball bounced over the ledge. Duke leaped over the side after it and was gone.

Just then Marianne walked into the apartment. Ralph said to her, "Hey, honey! Have you noticed your dog has been acting depressed lately?"

"Has your dog been acting depressed lately?"

Anderson, an armless man, sat down in a restaurant and asked for the manager. When he arrived Anderson had him order for him, feed him and wipe his face with a napkin. Then Anderson said, "I got to go to the toilet."

The manager led him to the men's room, took down his pants and left him sitting on the toilet. As the manager started to leave, Anderson shouted, "Did you hear a splash?"

"No," he said.

"You son-of-a-bitch," exclaimed the armless man, "you forgot to take my shorts down."

* * *

Peterson, a Vietnam vet, stood at a urinal. Because of bullet holes in his penis, the poor guy urinated all over another man standing beside him.

"I'm sorry," said Peterson, "but the doctors couldn't help me."

"The hell with the quacks!" exclaimed the drenched man. "Go to a piccolo teacher. He'll teach you to finger that stump so you won't piss all over strangers!"

"He lost both legs in a train wreck last year."

"Did the railroad treat him right?"

"He can't kick."

* * *

FIRE ISLAND POSTER
*Give now to wipe out the number-one
killer of all time: Natural Causes*

* * *

"Are you scared of flying?"

"No, it's the crashing that bothers me."

* * *

The passengers seated in the plane in flight heard this over the intercom system: "Sit back and relax. This plane is entirely automatic. Automatic pilot, automatic food servers, and automatic landing devices. You are perfectly safe. Enjoy your ride. Nothing can go wrong . . . go wrong . . . go wrong . . ."

* * *

You think you've got troubles? What about the deep-sea diver coming up who passed his ship going down?"

Cuatt, the traveling salesman, gave Kibler, an ignorant elderly farmer, a 50-pound case of Ex-lax as a present.

The old man ate it all in a few hours and died of the effects.

A month later Cuatt passed through town again and learned from the undertaker what happened.

"I'd like to leave some flowers on his grave," said the salesman.

"We ain't buried him yet. He's propped up in the outhouse. We're just waiting for him to get through!"

"*We're waiting for him to get through!*"

What's black and white and sees eye to eye?

Sammy Davis, Jr. and Moshe Dayan.

* * *

"You and your damned suicide attempts. Just look at this gas bill!"

* * *

SIGN OVER ELECTRIC CHAIR
YOU CAN BE SURE IF IT'S WESTINGHOUSE

* * *

It was a freak accident. He was run over by a truckload of dwarfs.

* * *

A young reporter, told to cut down the size of his news stories, wrote his next as follows:

"Eugene Stinehart looked up the shaft at the Royal Hotel this morning to see if the elevator was on its way down. It was. Age 25."

* * *

"Goodness, Glenn, this isn't our baby."
"Shut up! It's a better carriage."

Ronald was terriby deformed. In fact, he was just a head, with no body at all. But Ronald was a good boy and made his father proud of him.

Then, on his 21st birthday, his father took him out for his first drink. Ronald downed a shot of whiskey and made a face. But, suddenly, he began to grow a neck. He took another drink, and before long he had the beginnings of a chest. By the time he had finished the bottle, he was a strapping six-footer with a body of an Olympic wrestling champion.

"It's a miracle!" said his father, "Let's have one more drink to your good fortune."

The young man took another drink and vanished completely. His father just stared at the spot where he had been standing.

"Oh, well," he mused, "Ronald should have quit while he was a head."

*   *   *

"Did you know that in New York a man gets run over by a car every five minutes?"

"He must be mad as hell."

"I have a rather irregular request from that man in the dark cape," the blood bank attendant told his superior.

"What's that?" asked the boss.

"Well, sir," the attendant explained, "he wants two pints to go."

"I hate to tell you this, but your wife just fell in the well."

"That's OK, we use city water now."

*   *   *

"Understand your brother fell off a scaffold and died."

"That's right."

"I'm really sorry. What was he doing up there?"

"Getting hanged."

*   *   *

"I just saw a girl with a glass eye."

"How do you know? Did she tell you?"

"No. It came out in the conversation."

*   *   *

A sportsman went out into the woods with his dog and his gun. At the end of the day, he returned empty-handed. A friend asked, "Didn't you shoot anything?"

"I shot my dog."

"Was he mad?"

"He wasn't exactly mad, but he wasn't exactly pleased either."

DEPRESSION DITTY

I love life and life loves me,
I'm as happy as can be.
A happier man nowhere exists . . .
I think I'll go and slash my wrists.

* * *

The patient with high blood pressure was worried. "Tell me, Doc," he asked. "Just how sick am I?"

"Let me put it this way," said the doctor. "If it wasn't for your skin, you'd be a fountain."

* * *

Mrs. Gilbert was telling her husband that she had put her first-aid lessons to good use that afternoon.

"I was crossing Main Street," she said excitedly, "when I heard a terrific crash. There was a man lying in the middle of the street. He had been thrown through the windshield of his car. He had a compound fracture of the leg, a fractured skull, and was bleeding heavily. Quick as a flash, all my first-aid training came back to me. I sat down on the curb and put my head between my knees to keep from fainting."

"I know you're a hunchback, darling, but before you meet Mother, do try to straighten up a little."

"Please straighten up!"

POSTER IN BUS STATION
In case of atomic attack,
stay away from all windows,
loosen clothing,
get under a table or desk,
put your head between your legs,
and kiss your ass goodbye

*   *   *

"Does anyone aboard this submarine know how to pray?"

"I do."

"Good. You pray. The rest of us will put on escape lungs. We're short one."

*   *   *

"Do you realize, Frank, that this room we rented is supposed to be haunted by a ghost that returns every year on this date at midnight to find a human sacrifice? ... Frank? Frank!"

*   *   *

Did you hear about the ghoul who sent his girl a heart for Valentine's Day ... still beating?

Metcalf approached little Tyler sitting on a street corner.

"Say b-b-b-boy, c-c-could you direct me t-t-t-to the fire station?"

Tyler looked up at him and said nothing but slowly shook his head.

"L-L-Look here, are you s-s-s-sure you c-c-can't direct m-m-m-me to the fire station?"

Tyler looked up again and slowly nodded his head.

"W-W-Well, thank y-y-y-you anyway," said Metcalf and walked away.

Barker, standing nearby, overheard the whole conversation, walked up and glared at Tyler.

"Boy," he said, "why didn't you tell that man where the fire department is? You've been living in this town all your life, haven't you?"

"Yeah," answered the boy, "b-b-b-but do y-y-you think I w-w-wanna get the h-h-h-h-hell s-s-slapped out of m-m-m-me?"

*　　*　　*

What is a sadist?

A sadist is a person who is kind to a masochist.

Dennis Pinney tells about Harrison who was hurt in a motorcycle accident. His bike was totally demolished and Harrison wound up in the hospital. He lay completely bandaged up, in bed listening to the doctor.

"I've got good news and bad news for you," said the M.D.

"Give me the bad news first," said Harrison.

"I'm afraid," said the M.D., "I had to amputate both your feet."

"Oh, God," sobbed Harrison. "What's the good news?"

"The fellow in the next bed wants to buy your boots!" said the doctor.

"He wants to buy your boots!"

SIGN OF HAPPINESS
*Life is what you're doing while
you're waiting to die*

* * * *

Adolf Hitler was discovered hiding in Buenos Aires by two aged Nazis who told him he must take over Germany.

"But I'm a fugitive," he protested.

"We can fix everything," they said. "You must do it for the Fatherland."

Hitler thought it over. "All right, for the Fatherland I'll do it," he said. "But this time, no more Mr. Nice Guy."

* * *

Flanagan came home drunk one night. He could not negotiate the stairs to the second story of his house and passed out somewhere in the middle of the ascent. When he awoke, he heard his wife and two children in the kitchen. They couldn't have gotten there without passing his prostrate form, so he made it a point to ask them later why they didn't wake him up. The younger son's answer cleared things up.

"We thought," explained the eight year old, "that you was dead."

Did you hear about the frustrated hypochondriac who found out he was allergic to medicine?

* * *

A fellow with a one-foot man sitting on his shoulder walked into a bar and ordered a Scotch and soda. The bartender was stunned but delivered the drink as ordered. Just as the fellow was about to drink it, the little man knocked it out of his hand. He ordered another one, and again the little man knocked the drink onto the floor. This scene was repeated three times. Finally, the bartender could stand it no longer.

"What's going on here?" he asked.

"It's a long story," the man said, "but many years ago I was in Egypt and found a magic lamp. I rubbed it and a genie offered me three wishes. First I wished for ten million dollars. Then I wished for everlasting life."

"Sounds great," said the bartender. "What was your third wish?"

"I wished for a prick twelve inches long."

209

Langley said to his wife, "This bell is used only for emergencies. Now, I'm going out in the field and if anything like an Indian attack happens, ring the bell."

So the Old West settler went off to plow and a couple of minutes later the bell started ringing. Langley hurried to the house screaming, "What's the matter?"

"I thought I saw an Indian," said his wife.

He said, "The bell is only for real important things." So he went back out to work.

Suddenly the bell began peeling. He rushed back to the house.

"I made some cookies and thought you'd like some," said Mrs. Langley.

"I told you, don't ring the bell unless something really happens."

Langley went back to the field. Thirty minutes later the bell started ringing again. He ran back to the house and saw that it was on fire and his wife lay dead with an arrow in her back.

"Now this is more like it," said the settler.

"Now that's more like it!"

A waitress became violently ill while at work and was rushed by ambulance to the local emergency hospital. In typical hospital fashion, she was placed on an examining table and then all but ignored for the next half-hour. Finally, she noticed a doctor out in the hall and yelled, "Please help me!"

"Sorry," he replied, "it's not my table."

*   *   *

What do you do with a dog that has no legs?

Take it for a drag.

*   *   *

Michael picked up a blonde at a bar and after quite a few drinks, they went to a hotel room and made love. In the middle of the night Michael woke up to go to the bathroom, and noticed that the woman had taken off a wooden leg and laid it by the bed.

As the girl slept Michael began fiddling with its springs and braces, and finally found he had taken the wooden leg apart and could not put it back together again.

He went out into the hall, and stopped a man perfumed with booze, saying, "Can you help me? I've got a woman in my room with one leg apart, and I can't seem to get it back together."

"Hell!" said the drunk, "I got a woman in my room with *both* legs apart, and I can't even find the goddamn room!"

* * *

"He lost both legs in a train wreck last year."

"Did the railroad treat him right?"

"He can't kick."

* * *

At four o'clock one morning the Madame was most surprised to hear the doorbell ring. Yawning, she opened the door and stared at a man who had no arms or legs.

"I want a woman," he stated.

"Why don't you go on home, my girls have all turned in for the night."

"Look, lady, I want a woman now!"

"Hey, what do you think you could do with a woman in your condition?"

"I rang the bell, didn't I?"

Jerri Blandon from Los Angeles sent in this blissful bauble:

Did you hear about the man who was trampled to death in Disneyland?

He had an epileptic fit and everyone jumped on. They thought it was a new ride!

*　*　*

Harry was jaded and wanted something really different. The madame at the bawdy house remembered that Gloria had a glass eye, which when removed ...

It cost Harry $200, but it was a great experience. Afterwards, he thanked Gloria and gave her a $50 tip.

"Say, Gloria," asked Harry. "Would it be too sick to suggest that we do this again sometime?"

"Naw. It was sorta fun," she yawned.

"I'll come back next week, then," he said.

"Good," replied Gloria. "I'll keep an eye out for you."

DO NOT READ WHILE EATING

The following joke has my vote as the vilest, most disgusting in this collection. If you have a weak stomach, do not read it. Remember, I warned you:

Welles and Link were lost in the desert and hadn't eaten in weeks. Suddenly they stumbled on a dead coyote covered with maggots.

Welles, at the point of starvation, couldn't control himself. He fell on the decaying animal and began eating. Ten minutes later, he threw up all over the place.

At that moment, Link began eating what his friend had just vomited. But he stopped for a moment and said, "I knew if I waited long enough I'd have a hot meal!"

* * *